DIFFICULT QUESTIONS, EASY ANSWERS

DIFFICULT QUESTIONS, EASY ANSWERS

ROBERT GRAVES

CASSELL · LONDON

CASSELL & COMPANY LTD
35 Red Lion Square, London WC1R 4SG
SYDNEY, AUCKLAND, TORONTO,
JOHANNESBURG

First published 1972

I.S.B.N. 0 304 29091 2

Printed in Great Britain by
The Camelot Press Ltd, London and Southampton
F.972

Foreword

Every now and then, since 1931, I have published random collections of my shorter prose-pieces with or without verse additions:

But It Still Goes On (*1930 London, 1931 New York*)
The Common Asphodel (*1949 London*)
Occupation; Writer (*1950 New York, 1951 London*)
¡Catacrok! (*1956 London*)
Steps (*1958 London*)
Five Pens in Hand (*1958 New York*)
Food for Centaurs (*1960 New York*)
Mammon and the Black Goddess (*1965 London, New York*)
The Crane Bag (*1969 London*)

It is likely enough that this will be the last.

R. G.

Contents

1

Address to the Poets of Hungary

Budapesth, 1970

There are, I believe, only three countries in Europe
where the name of poet is everywhere honoured rather
than ridiculed. First comes Ireland, where for over two
thousand years the master-poet was also the historian,
doctor, musician, magician, prophet, Chief Justice and
Counsellor to the King—and ranked high above soldiers
and sailors. Next, Wales, where the poetic tradition
of the Eisteddfod or National Poetic Congress has out-
lasted even the English conquest. Finally Hungary. I
am Irish by birth, Welsh by adoption, and Hungary
has always brought me good luck, I suppose also because
of its outstanding poetic tradition. Why are there
about twenty times more poems written and published
in Hungary per head of the population than in any
other country? Hungary has survived conquest and
enslavement not by the help of religion or politics but by
poetry—as in Ireland and Wales. Hungarian poets have,
however, a quality unmatched by any other European
race—their language and their myths being completely
different from any other. Thus they cannot get lost
under the domination of neighbouring powers, few of
whose citizens ever take the trouble to learn Magyar.
Hungarians, like the ancient Irish and Welsh, realize
that poetry is a *means of storing power*: notably the
magical power of love. There are three forms of such
love: brotherly love, especially when poets are bound to
a certain town or profession or craft—or to their native
country. Then there is the physical love of poetic courtship which slowly merges into marital love. Lastly,
there is the poetic love which, though taking its language

from that of courtship, transcends the sexual link and is used by lovers for performing practical miracles of healing or for bringing about victories over evil powers against seemingly impossible odds. The word *poetry* in Greek has this very sense: poetry (*poisēis*) meaning making something remarkable happen. The Scots use the work *maker* for poet, but often spell it *makar* which in Greek is *makarios* meaning 'blessed' or 'happy'. The Greek origins of poetry are well known from the opening lines of Homer's two epics, the *Iliad* and the *Odyssey*. One begins: 'Sing to me, Muse', and the other 'Tell me, Muse'. This is a reminiscence of the ritual dance to the great Mountain Goddess, at Tempe, Delphi or elsewhere, when her people were dancing around a tall *herm*, or stone pillar, waiting for the Mountain Goddess to take possession of one of their number and make her, or him, burst into poetic song in the metre of the music. Homer, as a guest at some king's palace, sits chanting his epic to the sound of his lyre. He is reminding his audience that the music of the dance, conducted by a chorus leader, had a hypnotic effect on everyone taking part. He is trying to create the same effect himself. Dance metre, continuously repeated, puts listeners into the hypnotic trance which is the top level of sleep and in which they do not think in everyday logic but in dream images. Both the poet and his listeners fall under the spell; and whether the mood is love, terror or a sudden deep understanding of the past or future, the experience is always something that no so-called 'prose poetry' can achieve. The difference between Muse poetry, which is the real sort, and literary or academic poetry, is whether the poet becomes truly entranced or whether he merely plays at being entranced. In my own view Homer is a true poet whereas Virgil is a literary pretender to poetry.

I have long been a student of mythology and find two

animals traditionally connected with poetry all the way from Ireland to China. One is the Crane, which I believe you Hungarians call *daru*, and the other is the Horse. In Greek mythology the Cranes are given credit for having inspired the God Hermes to invent the alphabet. In Ireland they are guardians of alphabetic secrets. Cranes, however, despite their sanctity are fast becoming extinct as marshes are drained. The last crane in the British Isles was shot in North Wales in 1906, the last disappeared from Majorca, where I live, at about the same time. The only country in Europe where Cranes are said to be still breeding is Hungary. Cranes were sacred to the Moon, probably because they combined the Moon's colours of white, red and black, and because they were associated with the Willow-tree. The Willow-tree has been sacred to the Moon since the time of the Babylonian goddess Lillith, who appears in Biblical tradition as Adam's first wife.

When I was last here in Budapest, I mentioned my extraordinary luck when I was a boy: the first Hungarian I ever met was Kordaly! I learnt songs of his which my father had translated, such as: 'Far and high, the Cranes give cry.' While there are still Cranes in Hungary (and while there are still Horses) poetry is bound to continue. The sanctity of the Crane appears in the Greek story of the poet Ibycus. While on his way to the theatre, at Corinth if I remember rightly, he was attacked and killed by robbers. While the performance was taking place in his absence a flight of Cranes visited the theatre and hovered over the heads of the murderers, who had by that time gathered there. The cry went up: 'These are the Cranes of Ibycus!' and the murderers at once surrendered.

And now about Horses. The supreme emblem of poetry in Greece was the winged Horse Pegasus which drank from a fountain well sacred to the Moon goddess, and called *Hippocrene* meaning 'the Horse's well'. And Pegasus appears again in Islam under the name of Burak, the winged Horse on which the Prophet Mohammed rose up into the sky from Jerusalem in a moment of poetic ecstasy. Romantic poetry throughout mediaeval Europe is associated with Chivalry and Chivalry means the riding of Horses. The Anglo-French romances of Chivalry are based on the adventures of the British King Arthur, a famous cavalry leader of late-Roman times, who lived long before the arrival of the Anglo-Saxon infantry.

Concurrent with the gradual disappearance of the Horse from agriculture and its supersession by agricultural machinery, the old poetic way of thinking and feeling is everywhere fast disappearing—which is one more sinister side of the dangerous and almost universal supersession of craft by technology. Poetry is rooted in the principles of craft, guided by inspiration.

The poetic power, the power to make things happen—as understood, for instance, by the mediaeval Irish master-poets and by their middle-eastern Sufi contemporaries—and I am sure also by Hungarian master-poets—raises simple love-alliances to a point where physical absence supplies living presence. Poetry is closely connected with higher mathematics, and these miraculous experiences can occur not only in the fourth dimension, where prison walls of the third dimension are easily cheated, but can also occur in the fifth dimension where time is as easily manipulated as space can be in the usual third dimension, and where seemingly impossible coincidences and so-called 'acts of God' occur almost as a matter of course. In poetry, the fifth-dimensional co-identification of lovers is truth rather than idealistic fancy.*

* After this address was over I was informed that the Horse and Crane are the national totem-animals of Hungary, which both surprised and did not surprise me.

2
Genius

This is an embarrassing subject. Genius is so irregular, disputed and uncontrolled a phenomenon that writing about it is as difficult as discussing unidentified flying objects. To have seen a U.F.O. oneself does not make the task any easier, especially if it has landed in one's own garden and little green men with antennae have emerged. But at least geniuses silently recognize one another by the very way that they come into a room and sit down.

The word genius in its modern sense first appeared in eighteenth-century England. This was presently exported to Germany, there blown up romantically and re-imported to England in the nineteenth century. It implied an incommunicable power of inventive thought found among a few, very unusual people who somehow did not depend on academic education for their discoveries or performances. Fielding first used the word so in his *Tom Jones* (1749): 'By the wonderful force of genius only, without the least assistance of learning. . . .' Genius in this sense is now contrasted with mere talent, which means the intelligent exploitation of discoveries made by genius.

Not long ago I overheard a group of American professors wondering about the small Greek State of fifth century B.C. Athens. It seemed impossible, they agreed, that an equal percentage of historically important figures could appear today in any part of the United States despite the recent massive increase of educational facilities. But why? they wondered. One of them hopefully suggested that the title 'genius' is too grudgingly awarded nowadays; so that most of the numerous first-class physicists working in the States, whose technical know-how would have staggered Pericles, Socrates, Plato, Alcibiades, Aeschylus, Sophocles, Euripides, Anaxagoras, Zeno and all the other Athenian geniuses, are denied the title. But these professors seemed to me to be confusing historical importance with scientific talent, and scientific talent with the unfathomably original way of thought now associated with genius. For example Franklin, Watt, Marconi and Edison were men of unusual scientific talent, and attained considerable historical fame; whereas Clerk Maxwell, Rowan Hamilton, Thompson (of the genes) and Rutherford, whose work displayed all the signs of genius, remain almost unknown to the general public. Periclean Athens, of course, fascinates modern Americans. Pericles first democratized Athens by breaking the power of the ancient religious aristocracy and glorified his own name by an expansion of the Athenian fleet and colonial empire; also by fostering academic art, industry and commerce.

Yet I associate genius with the Athens of Pericles largely in a negative sense. His mercilessly dictatorial government, however neatly disguised as democracy, implied the exploitation of a large, industrious slave class and the deliberate rejection of ancient religious myths which had hitherto guided the social conscience, in favour of an over-simplified political logic. He made Athens a loveless city of agnostics, famed for its prestige architecture, statuary and philosophy, and sadly lacking in political honour.

Plato, who was born two years before Pericles's death, proved himself a notorious enemy of genius by barring poets from his ideal republic: I suppose it was because poetry at its most intense and memorable transcends logic that he dismissed it as 'madness'. Even today the dead hand of Plato compels students to think logically; and as more and more universities are losing their independence through being financed by the State or business corporations, the more and more logical does the educational system become. This illiberal trend explains the marked decline in native American genius since the turn of the century; for Platonists hold that nothing which cannot be logically proved is true, and this includes genius.

The original sense of *genius* was a far simpler mystery to accept and handle than the present one. The word *genius* is not Greek but Latin. Other Latin words of the same formation are *progenitor*, *generate*, *engender* and *genitals*. But *genius* had a spiritual rather than a physical sense and implied the primitive creative power with which a man is born and which accompanies him throughout life as his highest spiritual self, his protector, his oracle. A Roman who behaved evilly or foolishly was said to have 'defrauded his genius'. Genius was his primitive male dignity, his sense of love, and his power of instinctive thought, the preservation of which was his constant duty. Because such genius was considered noble and inspiring, the adjective *generous*, which in Latin implied a family tradition of honourable dealing, was formed from it. A similar formation was *genial*, which implied the incessant and comforting radiations of genius on a man's equals and subordinates. Still another formation was *genuine*, meaning the authenticity of this power. Horatius's inspired defence of the Tiber bridge against the whole Etruscan army was quoted as a typical example of personal genius. The Greeks, however, rejected this concept by philosophically opposing the good genius with an evil one. The imported Greek notion of opposing demons fighting for the possession of a man's soul weakened the Roman's simple confidence in a mystic power which took possession of him in times of crisis.

spiritual guardian which can foreknow and deliver the otherwise impossible and which goes straight to the answer without recourse to logical argument or its equivalent in mathematics or music. It appears that man in his gradual ascent from rudimentary forms of life has elaborated successive mechanisms of thought, the most recent and by no means the most effective of these being the logical use of cause and effect which is solidly linked with the cramping notion of measurable time and now rules the materialistic world.

In sleep, the mind reverts to primitive thought-mechanisms that occur on increasingly deeper levels, from light trances to so profoundly drugged a condition that its dreams convey images untranslatable to the waking intelligence. Sudden reversion in waking up to a pre-hominoid level of thought, as the result, for example, of shock caused by a block-busting explosion, can send a group of professional men scrabbling for escape on a tiled floor, rather than, as would happen under a lesser shock, merely running away or throwing hysterics. Some of us inherit primitive sensibility to signs of danger which evade our educated senses, but of which cats, dogs and horses are often conscious; others are from time to time granted clear visions of future events, ghosts of ancient history, or happenings at a distance, no doubt induced by an equally primitive thought-mechanism. Yet all such psychic phenomena are rejected by scientists because plainly not subject to repeatable experiment.

Below the rational level of consciousness, then, lie dream-levels. The deeper the sleep, the more difficult it is for the dreamer, on waking, to recall his dreams; their archaic imagery confuses him. It has now been agreed that the need to sleep is simply the need to dream: in other words the need to store up the day's conscious experience by translating it into dream language for one's memory files. When one sleeps on a problem and

wakes up with a satisfactory answer, personal genius
has obviously been at work and has diagnosed the
situation. Bad dreams are warnings that danger is
about; the genius has pricked up his ears at some element
which the rational mind had missed. The trance into
which a genius falls during the creative act gives him
access to the whole treasure-house of personal and
inherited memory. Since modern abstract painting began
as an attempt to recover and record genuine dream-
experience, a non-figurative painter is not necessarily
the impostor that logicians assume. But neither do his
paintings deserve to be described as 'pure art'—art
being by tradition informative—if they record personal
messages which have lost their coherence even for
himself. Genius will thus include the power to interpret
a dream that would seem absolute nonsense if told,
out of context, at the breakfast table.

When Kekulé von Stradonitz (1828–96) made his
most sensational chemical discovery it came to him in
comic dream form. As I wrote in the *Marmosite's
Miscellany* (London, 1925):

The maunderings of a maniac signifying nothing
I hold in respect; I hear his tale out.
Thought comes often clad in the strangest clothing:
So Kekulé the chemist watched the weird rout
Of eager atom-serpents writhing in and out
And waltzing tail to mouth. In that absurd guise
Appeared benzine and anilin, their drugs and their dyes.

Plato was worried by the logical crux that if we know the
solution of a problem then there is no problem; whereas
if we do not know the solution we do not know what
to look for and therefore cannot expect to find it. After
stating this in the *Meno*, Plato concluded that the solu-
tions of problems involves memory of pre-incarnations

11

in which the answers have already been found. How logical and how inept! The truth seems to be that genius is capable at some primitive thought-level of thinking in the fourth and fifth dimensions. In the fourth dimension one can explore the interior of a sealed chamber without breaching its walls. In the fifth, one is no longer bound by time but can see things happening in the past or future as easily as, for instance, if seated at ease in an aeroplane flying faster than clock time, one can watch the setting sun slowly rise again above the sea-horizon. One is also, it seems, capable of communing with other minds in the past, present or future. The creative act of poetry is fifth-dimensional in the sense that a poet catches at the nucleus of a poem, a single half-remembered phrase, and works at it until every line corresponds as nearly as possible with his foreknowledge of how the completed poem would be. Creative genius in dancing or music follows much the same principles.

In 1958 I visited the Weizmann Institute at Tel Aviv. Professor Sonnerschein asked me what I thought of his computer. I answered that we had not yet established any contact; it was busy with a spectroscopic job on helium rays. He assured me solemnly: 'This machine can do all that the human brain is capable of doing and better!'

It came into my mind to ask: 'Can it ordain cosmic coincidence?'

Professor Sonnerschein did not seem particularly taken aback by the question, but I had a suspicion that he did not quite understand what I meant. At any rate he answered politely: 'Not yet!'

I was asking, as matter of fact, whether this huge, complicated and costly dingbat could think in the fifth dimension, as geniuses can, discover the answer to a problem by proleptic thought and then discover the problem itself by analeptic thought. Cosmic coincidence is a simple fifth dimensional manipulation of time for making events concur against all statistical probability.

Mathematics as a field of abstract thought, rather than of Pythagorean magic, conveys so limited a sense of personal blessing and its adepts enter regions so far abstracted from common humanity that they tend to forfeit a necessary ingredient of genius, namely love. Mathematic genius is also notoriously short-lasting—it reaches a peak at the age of about twenty-three and then declines—and is as a rule coloured by persistent emotional adolescence. Since advanced mathematicians are too easily enticed into the grey political underworld of nuclear physics, a remarkably high percentage of mental breakdowns among their wives is everywhere noted.

Psychopaths are often mistaken for geniuses. The most common psychopath is the confidence trickster. The prisons are full of con-men; so are politics. Their power to read a victim's mind and so take advantage of his weaknesses is fortunately counterbalanced by their megalomania. Every con-man or political rabble-rouser tricks himself in the end. Alexander the Great, Napoleon and Hitler have been hailed as geniuses; but all were psychopaths conning themselves with their own boastful legends until they ruined their own countries and died shamefully with no sons to succeed them. So also perhaps was golden-tongued Pericles, who savagely oppressed his slaves, condoned outright massacre in the Greek island of Mytilene and elsewhere, and relying on his immensely powerful fleet, challenged the Spartans, his neighbours, to war. They began raiding Athenian territory, burning crops and huts, felling olive trees, driving away stock; and Pericles, all too logically, built the famous 'Long Walls' from the city down to the port of Piraeus, so that Athens became a secure and easily defended fortress. But one of his ships, trading in the East, brought back rats with bubonic plague. The crowded semi-siege conditions behind those famous 'Long Walls' fostered an epidemic which carried off a great part of the population, including (by what the tragedians would have called poetic justice) Pericles himself. Julius Caesar at least was no psychopath. He had a heart, courage, mercy, a sense of humour, Roman genius and remarkable humility; and though he fought with no holds barred when his life was threatened, kept faith with his real friends, had the future of his country at heart and knew its weaknesses.

Genius not only diagnoses a situation by non-logical thought but supplies the remedy. A horse-and-buggy doctor in the good old days would identify a disease first with his nose—one sniff was usually enough as he entered the sick-room—then with his ears, then with his eyes, then with his touch. He could as a rule dispense with a fever chart. Few of that breed survive. Today most general practitioners have lost the sense of smell from having spent so much of their medical training in cities where smell, taste and hearing soon degenerate. Though only the other day our Spanish village doctor cried out to a patient: 'Your breath smells of new-mown hay. That means pneumonia. To the hospital at once!' Diagnosis, for them, depends on text-books; yet as a rule these say nothing about that almost imperceptible twitch of an eyelid, that slight slurring in the patient's speech, that curiously sour whiff of sweat, which informed the horse-and-buggy doctor exactly what was amiss.

The mental deficients whom the French call *idiots savants* and who are classed as throwbacks to primitive hominoids, may have extraordinary mental gifts and, if they happen to inherit mathematic genes and are introduced to simple arithmetic will soon out-compute a computer. Being born, however, without any altruism or moral compunction, they resist training in humanity or in any work which brings them no immediate profit.

The Roman view of genius as guardian of the male creative process has much to commend it. Man's strongest concentration of mental power occurs when he falls in love. The gonad glands control this impulse, but in the course of millennia the power of love has become enormously extended and diversified. The first awareness of genius comes, it seems, with the common mystical experience of pre-puberty, in which a child is convinced that he knows everything or can do everything and keeps his illusion for some hours. Since this experience can be related to the first active awakening of his gonads, we may presume a continued relation between gonad and genius. The relation however, tends to weaken whenever genius is defrauded: for example by the discovery of how much easier it is to steal than to earn, to cheat than to work, to lie than to tell the truth and to do whatever one pleases rather than obey one's conscience. Yet a recollection of this mystical assurance of suprahuman powers and a belief in its basic reality will, I believe, support whoever dares make that sudden leap in the dark, that escape from the tyranny of time, which fifth-dimensional genius implies.

A remarkable contemporary genius, Sir Macfarlane Burnet, the Australian biologist, began his investigations by a poetic opposition of the self and the non-self. How does the self recognize non-self and expel it from the body? Sir Macfarlane Burnet's answer was that the self occasionally makes mistaken experiments that defraud its own genius and set chemical bodies acting against the body's component cells. This view has at last made such diseases as rheumatoid arthritis intelligible to biologists and led to a startling new concept of immunity. One can now study which cells control the self's defences, and how they do it. The non-self is not however a built-in evil genius, as the Greeks would have seen it, but, as the Romans would have seen it, an invader. The principle of immunity is, roughly, that the self despatches a cell to take stock of the non-self, find out what it is projecting, and then return and advise its fellow-cells exactly what chemical repellent to manufacture for spreading over these projections. They keep on at this task until they have manufactured enough for their purpose; which explains the two-to-three or seven-day period of an illness, followed by rapid recovery.

'Genius' was a word loosely used by expatriot Americans in Paris and Rome, between the Versailles Peace treaty and the Depression, to cover all varieties of artistic, literary and musical experimentalism. A useful and readable history of the literary Thirties is *All Geniuses Together* by Kay Boyle—Joyce, Hemingway, Scott Fitzgerald, Pound, Eliot and the rest. They all became famous figures but too many of them developed defects of character—ambition, meanness, boastfulness, cowardice or inhumanity—that defrauded their early genius. Experimentalism is a quality alien to genius. It implies doubt, hope, uncertainty, the need for group reassurance; whereas genius works alone, in confidence of a foreknown result. Experiments are useful as a demonstration of how not to write, paint or compose if one's interest lies in durable rather than fashionable results; but since far more self-styled artists are interested in *frissons à la mode* rather than in truth, it is foolish to protest. Experimentalism means variation on the theme of other people's uncertainties.

Winston Churchill, whom I knew off and on, from 1916 until 1948, had escaped the educational routine that inhibited so many of his university trained fellow politicians. After a bad start at school, his family connections admitted him into the cavalry, where he educated himself. His was an inconsistent genius, frequently

16

defrauded by political commitments; but his courage, humour, generosity and loyalty to his friends were beyond exception. I once met Lloyd George, Churchill's one-time colleague, and national hero of the first World War: a rabble-rouser with a golden voice and little personal honour who passed for a genius during the first World War. Having plotted against his colleague, Asquith, he seized power from him, kept the war going at enormous cost of life and treasure for two years longer than necessary, left his country all but bankrupt, and at Versailles helped to sow the seeds of a second, still more disastrous war.

After a brief glimpse of Einstein at Princeton in 1929, I could not doubt the early genius which corresponded with his later humility, kindliness and sense of humour. His theory of relativity had been classical and humane, and his Universe made good geometrical sense, however startling at the time. But science has broken through into a post-classical phase of algebraic thought so far beyond practical human apprehension that the cosmic observations summarized by computers make no intelligible terrestrial sense. Though this obviously wholesome limit set on human thought may one day encourage a reappraisal and reform of human society, at present it is tempting advanced scientists to despise all creative human values. How many of these ratiocinatory cosmonauts have defrauded their genius is shown by the shambles that they make of their private terrestrial lives and their readiness to encourage terrestrial nuclear warfare. That warfare is a natural human function need not be disputed—most young men are pugnacious—yet I agreed with T. E. Lawrence when he told me that war ceased to be human at the battle fought at Crécy in August 1346, where the English first used artillery on a battlefield. Military genius has now come to be a contradiction in terms; all modern wars are fought with pitiless logistics, with scientific poisoning of the enemy's land and water, and with a singular absence even of military talent.

Student riots all over the world seem symptomatic of an approaching change in the modern way of life; since the focus of disorder is almost always the philosophic department of a university. They are a natural reaction against the growing control of education by the political machine, big business, and a body of docile scientists who conduct experiments on lines laid down by their directors. The students are protesting, however blindly, in the name of genius against its antonym, against Logic, and in clear agreement with Plato's enemy the sophist Protagoras that 'man' (meaning, as he explained, man with an inborn sense of justice, nobility and holiness) 'is the measure of all things'. Also incidentally, the students are protesting against individualistic wars fought against ideal communism (which after all is no more than a different theory from ours as to who should direct the flow of money and control) and fought in direct contravention of international agreements about permissible means. Male students in these riots, now sporadic throughout the non-Communist world, are more active fighters than their girl friends who, as a rule, are content merely to incite. Yet lately in Mexico just before the Olympics opened, I learned that on four separate occasions, a couple of 'Bonnies' had assisted their 'Clydes' by the same stratagem. The pair would wait for the approach of a single unsuspecting police officer and then start ripping each other's clothes off, tearing out each other's hair and screaming abuse. When he gallantly tried to separate them, out would come their daggers and slide into his lungs or stomach. Dirty work, but Jael, Delilah and Judith had set the Biblical precedent. . . . It is indeed women who stand to lose most by a further strengthening of the mechanically

directed and computed thought which tends to hasten
men's physical impotence—a phenomenon now reported
at an increasingly premature age among steady-going
married executives.

Romans refused to credit women with an individual
genius, on the grounds that they did not engender but
parturiated: and held them, instead, to lie under the
divine guidance of the goddess Juno Lucina. This
implied that men were ruled by a male code, but women
by a divinity which absolved them of obedience to any
code at all, except that of being true to their own bodies.
And though a patrician Roman's appetite might casually
involve him with women from whom he declined to
breed children, his social conscience opposed a similar
instinct in his female relatives. Roman women at first
accepted the practical value of this ban on their sleeping
with men who lacked the generous tutelary power of
patrician genius; but by Catullus's time female morals
had noticeably relaxed. The goddess Juno Lucina, as he
reminds us, was not only the wife of Almighty Jupiter
and the protectress of women in childbirth; she was
also, as her second name proved, the powerful, enchant-
ing, lecherous, perpetually virgin Moon-goddess—hun-
tress, prophetess and healer.

Western High Society still deprecates *mésalliances*,
but wherever acceptable alliances are judged not merely
by a man's wealth, influence and talents, but by his
integrity, women too often make trouble by falling in
love with outsiders whom their fellow men recognize
as cads or crooks. The male proverb 'no woman is wise
below the girdle' is, of course, a libellous exaggeration;
but few married women like to be cheated of satisfaction
in what the Romans called 'the genial couch', meaning
the marriage bed. Moreover, in choosing their lovers,
few women of spirit realize that a man who has forfeited
his sense of honour by some disgraceful act can never be

19

redeemed by even a perfect woman's love. That women themselves are infinitely redeemable makes it hard for them to realize that what the Romans called 'a lost man', meaning that he had assassinated his genius, is like a drinking glass, which however neatly repaired after breakage will never again ring clear when tapped with the finger nail. On the other hand, I wrote once about a woman-friend of mine:

She is no liar, yet she will wash away
Honey from her lips, blood from her shadowy hand,
And, dressed at dawn in clean white robes will say,
Trusting the ignorant world to understand:
'Such things no longer are; this is today.'

That was written not in anger: I was merely echoing the text of *Proverbs* XXX, 20.

Under normal semi-civilized unmechanized conditions, a man's physical metabolism changed so little from the age of about fifteen to eighty that his genius was held to remain with him until he became incapable of generation, and took to the chimney-corner. Thus in *Deuteronomy* XXXIV, 7, Moses was extolled as having kept his virility and eyesight until he died on Mount Pisgah at the age of 120. By contrast, not only does a woman go through a dramatic change both at puberty and after reaching her menopause in middle age—Sarah who gave birth to Isaac at the age of ninety was a remarkable exception!—but during each pregnancy the presence of her unborn child, which has different genes from her own, will noticeably affect her character. However, even throughout her nubile period, any unspoilt woman is capable of using her mind in the timeless, nonchalant way characteristic of genius: which is to make extraordinary complicated problems seem as simple as counting on one's fingers—by the manipulation of time.

And women are granted the mystical pre-puberty experience of 'knowing everything' as often as boys; I have even known one who had it under an anaesthetic during the birth of her first daughter.

I once wrote of a woman genius:

> If strange things happen where she is
> So that men say that graves open
> And the dead walk, or that futurity
> Becomes a womb and the unborn are shed,
> Such portents are not to be wondered at,
> Being tourbillions in Time made
> By the strong pulling of her bladed mind
> Through that ever-reluctant element.

In real love, as opposed to confused sexual groping or a simple decision to marry and settle down, genius is always present; and manifests itself with its usual supra-sensory bending of time into a manageable ring. Only a few advanced students have become aware of this phenomenon, which they account for in terms of a concept named *Omega Minus*, but of which being professionally free of the tender passion, they claim no personal experience.

One thing more. If ever one is suddenly threatened by extreme danger while bed-ridden the protective genius should immediately come to his rescue. I am reminded of this by my great-uncle Dr. Robert Graves whose statue sits in marble in the Irish College of Physicians at Dublin. He was once confined by fever to his cabin in a small Greek ship as it was rounding the Peloponnese. A huge storm blew up. Hearing cries, curses and stamp-ings overhead, he forced himself to climb on deck, and found that the crew had decided to abandon ship. His practised eye told him that the ship's boat which they were about to lower overboard could not possibly survive such a sea, so he picked up a cannon ball, lifted it high above his head and hurled it through the boat's side. The crew, thus forcibly deprived of escape, came to their senses and somehow brought the ship into harbour.

In the first World War trenches the protective power of genius was daily proved. I cannot recall a single man with a running nose or a cough, in spite of the fearful cold and damp and the lack of protective clothing. So long as morale was high—and it was my duty as a company officer to keep it high—danger kept us alert and in good health. Yet after six or seven months of continuous shelling our adrenalin glands over-compensated against the continuous nervous pressure of noise and we gradually lost our power of immediate reaction to danger. Although illness can result from distress at watching the oppressive effects of modern living on too many of our neighbours, sympathy with their sufferings should urge our genius into action—a cannon ball hurled through the boat—rather than keep us lying hopelessly on our bunks.

3
Arts and Crafts

Art (*ars* in Latin) is connected with the Greek word *artao*, to 'join together', meant in fact what we now call *craft* in the sense of 'smith-craft' or handicraft, and produced the word *arma* (arms) especially for such defensive arms as shield and helmet.

Craft originally meant 'active strength and power'. Both words have degenerated under improper usage: 'crafty' came to mean dishonest manipulation of a situation, as 'artful' also did.

The main difference between them is now, roughly, that craft is expected to produce useful objects and art to produce pleasing effects. In the English Middle Ages the craft-guilds consisted of masters, journeymen and apprentices. After ten or twelve years of subservient apprenticeship to a Master who taught him his craft— of working in wood, metal, fur, cloth or whatever else it might be—the apprentice became an independent journeyman, working for wages. Eventually he might qualify to become a Master by submitting a piece of handicraft made by himself to the inspection of the senior Guild Masters. This was called a 'masterpiece'.

'Masterpiece' is now incorrectly used to mean a work of art that excites wonder: it should mean no more than a work showing a high degree of craftsmanship. There has been no guild of painters, or sculptors, musicians or dancers in England powerful enough to be represented at the Guildhall. Apprenticeship in the arts has therefore remained unregulated until recently when such institutions as the Royal Ballet School, the Royal College of Music and the Slade School of Art were endowed.

Successful students graduate as masters (or mistresses) of their profession; but even after learning their craft to their teachers' satisfaction, can they claim to excite wonder?

'Craftsman' remains an honourable word even since the crumbling away of the guild system: it means a man who knows how to handle the tools of his craft rather than be part of an industrial machine which does the precision work for him. 'Artist' is a word that has gone downhill so irrevocably that it has for some years been used as a term of mockery among professional painters, sculptors and draughtsmen.

4

The Bible in Europe

In the early seventh century A.D. the prophet Mohammed ordered his Faithful to respect all peoples who worshipped God according to their own sacred Scriptures, as the Faithful themselves must obey the Koran which God had inspired him to write. This order ensured religious liberty to Jews throughout Islam; and to all Christians (however violently they might disagree among themselves on the interpretation of Scripture) so long only as they made no attempt to convert Moslems to Christianity. On the other hand, all peoples who relied merely on popular myths or unwritten doctrine were treated as infidels and invited to choose between conquest or conversion to Islam. Christians were fortunate in having by that time agreed at least on a common text for their Bible. This consisted of two distinct parts: namely the Jewish Scriptures, renamed by St. Paul the 'Old Testament', as authorized for national use by the Jerusalem Supreme Court at the Council of Jamnia in A.D. 100, and the New Testament, selected Christian records of Jesus's life and of primitive Church history.

Faithfulness to their own Scriptures keeps the main body of religious Jews far more closely united than the Christians have ever been. This is because the historic and prophetic Books of the Old Testament, a bequest from their own ancestors, have been more carefully edited and co-ordinated than those of the New. The Koran enjoys much the same advantage: it was written in Arabic for Arabs, who took the language with them wherever they went in their wars of conquest, instead of adopting others. The Christian Bible, in contrast, suffers from a lack of linguistic cohesion. The Old Testament consists of ancient Hebrew texts translated into post-Classical Alexandrian Greek; and as for the Gospels, though Jesus and his disciples spoke Aramaic, a religious law in Judaea and Galilee forbade the recording, except in memory, of any religious teaching even by qualified teachers. The Gospels were therefore first written down, it seems, in Greek by Syrian converts whose dialect of Hebrew, called Syriac, varied greatly from Aramaic; this seems to have caused much misunderstanding. The separation of the Eastern and Western Churches caused further linguistic confusion. Most Easterners remained true to the Greek version; but Latin being the common language of the West, the Roman Church eventually adopted St. Jerome's Latin translation of both Old and New Testaments, completed in A.D. 405 and known as the Vulgate.

In the late fifth century, after the collapse of the Western Empire under barbarian pressure, correct Latin was gradually displaced by vernaculars throughout Europe; yet remained the language of religion, diplomacy and scholarship, becoming in fact aristocratic, as also did the Roman leadership of the Church despite its largely working-class origin. In contrast, the Jewish synagogue system preserved literary Hebrew as a common language of communication between Jews over a vast stretch of country from India and Babylonia to Spain, whatever their station or profession. Similarly, Moslems of all degrees communicated with one another in classical Arabic across an even wider stretch of country. Yet by the later Middle Ages few members of European land-owning families, unless they kept a private chaplain, could understand even the Latin Mass. Moreover the primitive Apostolic church had been communistic and even, to judge from Paul's frank account to the Galatians (*Galatians* II, 1–5) of his visit to Jerusalem in the year

A.D. 49, more or less anarchic. These were dangerous political trends which later it was thought prudent to disguise. Finally, the Bible lay under the great disadvantage, compared with the Jewish Scriptures and the Koran, of not being a national historic document. Its geographical names and the names of its leading characters conveyed little to non-Jewish converts, and being a translation of a translation of a translation, rather than an original text, it lacked the insistent poetic rhythms which made a great part of the Hebrew Scriptures, and all the Koran, easily memorizable.

All three monotheistic religions teach a stubborn faith in man's moral perfectibility; but the Christians are alone in holding that this cannot be brought about except by modelling one's conduct on that of Jesus— who laid down his life to save mankind from evil, whose birth inaugurated a new calendar, and whom they identify with God. Women are allowed a subsidiary part in the campaign to spread this faith around the world but, though on the whole far more devout than their men-folk, they have always been denied a part in the priesthood or a voice in Church councils. Christianity, like Judaism and Islam, is a stubbornly patriarchal religion. St. Clement of Alexandria, recalling the legend of Eve, wrote that every woman should be ashamed that she is born so.

Whether Jesus, when on earth, was man or God— and if God, how he could, as his Father's Son, rank as the only God—have been subjects of constant philosophical dispute among Christians, despite the Church's official adoption of the Trinity doctrine. Jesus is claimed in Luke as paternally descended from the heroic King David (*Matthew* I, 1, *Luke* III, 31); but a careful consideration of such Gospel texts as *John* XIX, 23 and *Matthew* XVII, 24–7 suggests that after his acclamation as the 'Messiah' or 'Christ'—both words meaning 'Anointed King'—by

27

John the Baptist, he was adopted into the priestly tribe of Levi. For three years, A.D. 27–30 he preached the gospel of repentance from sin. He addressed only Jews, and ordered his disciples similarly to avoid preaching in Gentile districts (*Matthew* x, 5), regarding all foreigners not yet wholly converted to the Mosaic Law as 'dogs' and 'swine' (*Mark* VII, 27, *Matthew* VII, 6). In those days, however, the later books of the Hebrew Scriptures which carried a prophetic message of love and of a heaven reserved for those who kept the Law, had not been accepted by the entire Jewish people. A Sadducee minority, consisting of endowed priests and their Levite assistants, confined its religious belief to the first five books of the Bible (the *Torah*, or *Pentateuch*) and the early historical books, rejecting the Prophets. Most of them were Roman collaborationists. It was on orders of the Sadducee High Priest—an Egyptian, not a Palestinian Jew—that Jesus was arrested in A.D. 30 as a pretender to the Throne of David and handed over to the Romans for trial.

Jesus was crucified at the request, it seems, of his pro-Roman enemy Prince Herod Antipas, a son of Herod the Great and Tetrarch of Galilee, Jesus's native province; the request being granted by Pontius Pilate, the local representative of the Emperor Tiberius, who supplied the executioners. Herod Antipas's hand was probably forced by his wife Herodias. John the Baptist had declared their marriage incestuous, and even before John's decapitation at Herodias's request, Jesus had been continuing his work of baptism (*John* III, 22) in the trans-Jordanian province of Peraea, which was threatened with war by Herod's former father-in-law, King Aretas of Nabatea. Herod Antipas now transferred his enmity from John to Jesus (*Luke* IX, 9, XIII, 31). This political background is soft-pedalled in the Gospels, because Herod was an ally of the Romans. The Jewish

Sanhedrin, or Supreme Court, consisting almost wholly of Pharisees, which (according to the Gospels) tried and found Jesus guilty, could not by its own religious rules have been convened on the Eve of the Passover, which was the day mentioned in the Gospels. Jesus's case will, instead, have come up before a Roman-appointed Sadducee advisory court, consisting of fifteen men led by the High Priest and his family. These had no authority to sentence anyone to death; and even the Sanhedrin Court, if they had found Jesus guilty, could have ordered no more than a severe flogging (*see* II *Corinthians* XI, 24) for his breach of the peace by cleansing the Temple Courts of money-changers. Nevertheless, early Gentile–Christian leaders preached that the Jewish nation had crucified Jesus, and that Pontius Pilate had done his best to spare his life—a historically untenable view which still lingers in popular superstition and in the English Coronation Service.

Church leaders had to protect their flocks from all suspicion of plotting against Rome; especially after the crushing defeat of the Jewish Revolt in A.D. 68, the subsequent dismantling of the Temple by the Emperor Titus, and the barbarous persecution of Jews not only in Palestine but throughout the whole Empire. To conceal John's illegal proclamation of an Anointed King seemed to the Gospel editors morally justifiable; in fact, devotion to Jesus's memory seemed sufficient excuse for further tampering with the records. The original facts were soon forgotten and cannot now be restored without difficulty. Since Jesus's installation as King of Israel would have needed the assent of the Emperor Tiberius and the Roman Senate, Christian leaders were at pains to disguise the implications of this rite, at which the Coronation Hymn seems to have been sung (*Mark* I, 10; *Psalm* II, 2), and the exalted Dove (Yahu)—which is said to be the original meaning of the word 'Jehovah'—

to have entered into him. They chose to represent his kingship as a spiritual event, devoid of all political significance.

The Pharisees, a high-minded and puritanical Jewish sect, whose religious rules Jesus ordered his disciples to follow (*Matthew* XXIII, 1–3) while at times condemning certain unworthy members of the sect—who because of St. Paul's later quarrel with them are consistently misrepresented by Gospel editors—agreed that one of Israel's worst calamities was when the seventy-two Jewish scholars of Alexandria translated the Hebrew Scriptures into Greek. This version, now called The *Septuagint* ('The Seventy'), is the basis of our Christian Old Testament. Its publication in the reign of King Ptolemy Philadelphus about the year 288 B.C. allowed a national religious document—the true meaning of which, it was held, only trained Doctors of the Law could expound—to be studied by ignorant foreigners who might, and did, quote its verses in ridicule of the Jewish Faith. Much the same complaint was made many centuries later by Roman Church authorities when the Vulgate, which few but priests could read, and which had indeed been put on the *Index*—the list of books that no ordinary Christian might read without priestly permission—was furtively translated into German, Dutch, English, and other vernacular languages. A great mass of uneducated people were thus freed to interpret the Scriptures as they pleased, and form dangerous new heretical sects. The Pharisees had been right in deploring the Septuagint. Without it, Christians would have persecuted no Jews; but, also, without vernacular Bibles there would have been no Lutheranism and no protracted religious wars fought between Catholics and Protestants.

The theme of the Jewish Scriptures had been a gradual refinement of religious practice from the earliest times until the appearance of Pompey's Roman forces in Palestine. The principles of the early historic books, originally inspired by Israelite devotion to the once savage pastoral god El, now appear abominable to idealistic Christians; yet the barbarity of God's chosen people when exterminating the Canaanite natives, as described in *Exodus* and *Joshua*, has been quoted by Christians ever since the Crusades as a licence for all ruthless wars of conquest. However, the early Christian editors had included these unhappy events in their Bible merely as contrasts with Jesus's wholly pacific gospel (*Matthew* XXVI, 52–3).

A main reason for the decline of church-going throughout the Western world, except where business firms prefer to recruit their executives from respectable members of some religious faith or other, is that so many supposedly scientific and historical facts contained in the Bible have long been disproved by experts. Unfortunately 'fundamentalism', meaning a literal acceptance of myths and metaphors used throughout the Bible, is a common disease of Christianity, and the honest agnostic who feels his mind becoming split into two irreconcilable parts, the religious and the practical, feels obliged to leave the Church for the protection of his sanity.

The song in the American musical *Porgy and Bess* is much to the point:

> It ain't necessarily so,
> It ain't necessarily so:
> The things that you're li'ble
> To read in the Bible,
> They ain't necessarily so.

For instance, Jacob's twelve sons and his sole daughter Dinah (*Genesis* XXX, 21) represented not the progeny of a single ancestor but twelve patriarchal tribes, and one matriarchal tribe, in an Israelite pastoral confederacy of the second millennium B.C. Jacob's quarrel with his elder brother Esau will have been a quarrel between this confederacy and an Edomite one which it drove south from disputed grazing grounds in Palestine. The whale that swallowed Jonah and then regurgitated him (*Matthew* XII, 40) is the story most often ridiculed by agnostics. No whale's throat, they say incorrectly, can admit the passage of even a small animal, let alone a man; nor does the Mediterranean provide enough plankton for a whale's diet. Yet the whale in *The Book of Jonah* is clearly a metaphor of the sea-power of Tyre and Sidon, Phoenician maritime cities lying to the north-west of Israel. The Jews possessed no navy and no deep-sea fisheries, and in Jesus's time a crossing of the sea made one ritually unclean. 'Jonah' clearly stands for Jews who had become separated from their religious cult-centre by involvement in Phoenician trade, but who changed their minds and returned home. Yet, for the fundamentalist, the whale remains a real whale, strayed into the Mediterranean from the Atlantic, by enlarging whose gullet and giving Jonah access to whose belly, God performed a miracle.

Fundamentalists also believe in the literal truth of how Joshua (*Joshua* X, 12) prayed for victory over the Amorites, whereupon God stopped the Sun in the western sky and forbade it to set for a whole day until the Israelites had won their battle. Yet the story is no more than a vivid way of recording that what promised to be two days of battle had to be finished in one, for fear that the Amorites might escape in the darkness. Similarly, Isaiah's prayer that God would lengthen King Hezekiah's life was followed by an apparent miracle: the turning back the shadow on a royal sundial (II *Kings*, XX, 11). This can have only been a simple example of sympathetic magic: Isaiah symbolically turned the whole sundial around in reverse.

The Seven Days of Creation (*Genesis* II, 3) are another stumbling block for well educated believers. Geologists have now shown that there was life on the earth a hundred million years or more before the first man appeared. In *Genesis*, however, 'days' are used as a metaphor for ages, such as those to which we now give such names as Tertiary, Jurassic, Cambrian and pre-Cambrian. I was once shown a tall cliff in the Negeb Desert of Israel, from the continuous strata of which can be read the geological history of the world back from Biblical times to the pre-fossil age. Even so, the metaphorical account in *Genesis* has a puzzling twist. 'Why,' doubters ask, 'did God create trees and grass before he created stars?' The historical answer is that a seven-branched candlestick was preserved in the Temple at Jerusalem—it figures among the triumphal trophies on the arch of the Emperor Titus at Rome—which according to the Jewish historian Josephus (*Antiquities* III, 7) represented the holy seven-day week. Each branch stood for a day sacred to one of the seven known planets: Sun, Moon, Mars, Mercury, Jupiter, Venus, Saturn. Astrologers from Babylon had ascribed different powers to each planet and worshipped them as deities. Their names varied from country to country. In Britain the weekdays have kept their Nordic names—the gods Woden (Odin) and Thor, the goddesses Tuisto and Frigg. Among the French, Spanish and Italians these days keep their Latin names in honour of the gods Mars, Mercury, Jupiter, Venus and Saturn. In Babylon, Tuesday was ruled by the Shepherd-god Nergal and the god of Wednesday was Nabu, the god of astrology. When, therefore, the Jews used their seven-branched candlestick in ritual celebration of an Almighty God who controlled all celestial powers, the planetary order of the seven branches was mistakenly held to conform with the Days of Creation. Hence in *Genesis* (the latest of the 'Five Books of Moses' to be recorded in writing) the invention of trees and grass needed by Nergal's shepherds was placed before the invention of Nabu's stars, although the order given in earlier Creation stories had been a more plausible one.

I have yet to find a Biblical story, however wildly it may read, that does not make at least metaphorical sense. For example, the manna (meaning 'what-is-it?') which the Israelites first ate in the desert of Sinai (*Exodus* XVI, *Numbers* XI) still forms on tamarisk bushes in the desert of Sinai—as it does in Australian deserts on 'wattles'. Manna resembles honey-dew, the sticky-sweet excretion of an aphid, which in northern Europe drips from linden-trees. Both manna and honey-dew, if left too long exposed to the weather, are subject to a hallucinogenic fungus, not unlike ergot which has recently been made the basis of lysergic acid. It was, it seems, because the fungus induced psychedelic visions that Moses forbade the Israelites to eat any but a daily allowance of fresh manna (*Exodus* XVI, 19). Yet because some of the eaters had enjoyed divine visions, a golden pot of manna was laid up in the Ark of the Covenant for the use of the priesthood alone (*Exodus* XVI, 33). Manna from Sinai, of which I was once given a taste from the end of a matchstick by the late President Ben Swi of Israel, became proverbial as a metaphor of God's enlightening mercy (*Deuteronomy* VIII, 3, *Nehemiah* IX, 20, *Psalm* LXXVIII, 24). Jesus himself used the metaphor in *John* VI, 31-6, and incorporated it in the Lord's Prayer, 'Give us today the bread of our daily allowance'—a reference to *Proverbs* XXX, 8, itself a reference to the account in *Exodus*. The unknown author of the Egypto-Greek *Book of Esdras*, which is included in the Biblical Apocrypha, seems to have been aware of the hallucinogenic properties of manna. In Book II of *Esdras* I, 19, he calls it 'angels' food', angels being concerned with divine inspiration. In the *Wisdom of Solomon* XIX, 21, it even appears as 'ambrosial food';* the Greek *ambrosia* ('divine') is now known to have been a fungal hallucinogene used in the rites of the god Dionysus, as *soma* was in those of the Vedic god Indra.

It is difficult to decide how literally Jews as a whole took these religious myths and metaphors; but we know that the Christian Church insisted almost from the start—although Jesus himself often spoke in the language of metaphor—on fundamentalism as a test of complete faith. Although this demand seemed no great obstacle to believers in pre-scientific days, it has increased heart-searchings in educated churchmen ever since. The Virgin Birth was already a stumbling-block in the early Roman Empire, although a similar miracle of divine birth had been accepted by the Greeks and Romans to account for the miraculous feats of such heroes as Hercules and Perseus. Another stumbling-block was Jesus's Ascension, although the hero Hercules's ascent to Heaven in a similar cloud from Mount Oeta in Greece had been widely accepted in the Graeco-Roman world. Yet scientifically-minded Greeks (who had invented the steam engine, predicted eclipses and correctly calculated the earth's diameter long before Jesus's time) rejected the literal truth of both these Christian legends—very much as they had mocked at their own. They will have known that the ancient Hebrew installation rights of an anointed king involved a ceremony of symbolic drowning called baptism, followed by his symbolic re-birth: passing under the skirts of a royal virgin and then changing his name. This ceremony was, it seems, of East African origin. Jesus's new name after the ceremony performed

---

* 'heavenly meat'—heavenly, literally 'ambrosial'.

by John seems to have been 'Netzer', meaning 'The Branch' (*Zechariah* III, 8, and VI, 12, and *Jeremiah* XXIII, 5). Yet the Christian writer Lactantius solemnly accounts for Jesus's Virgin Birth—caused according to Church doctrine, by inspiration of the Holy Spirit (*spiritus* in Latin means 'breath' or 'wind')—with a report that in Spain mares conceive by turning their hindquarters to the East Wind. Lactantius, in fact, took this Spanish fable literally, too, not as metaphorical of horses that run as fast as the wind. Jesus is given two genealogies in the Gospels (*Matthew* I, 1–16, *Luke* III, 23–38). The one in *Luke* is probably genuine; and ends with Joseph, who in the earliest existing Syriac Gospel manuscript, the *Codex Sinaiticus* in the British Museum, is said to have begotten him. This important fact was altered in Greek manuscripts, yet it is also found not only in the *Diatessaron*, but in *Acts* II, 30, *Romans* I, 3, *Hebrews* VII, 14, *Galatians* IV, 4–5. The *Luke* genealogy is suspect and seems to record Jesus's Levite ancestry tacked on to a genuine Davidic descent through Nathan. The Matthew genealogy is still more suspect, because it runs from David in the line through Rehoboam to Josiah, despite the curse laid on it by the prophet Jeremiah (*Jeremiah* XXII, 28–30; XXXVI, 30).

Christian missionaries persuaded their converts to believe in Holy Writ despite all reason; and represented the Devil as imperilling their salvation by his appeals to common sense. For the most part, however, the central message of Christianity, that of a loving God, was both new enough and important enough to make converts accept Biblical miracles as readily as they had accepted pagan myths. Nor could the Church now go back, without embarrassment, on its own doctrinal authentication of every chapter in the Bible as inspired by God and therefore literally true—even if, as in the case of Jesus's two genealogies, different passages plainly contradicted one another. To do so would, they said, be an offence against 'The Little Ones' who believed in Jesus (*Mark* IX, 42) and make them stumble. Thus the educated convert who underwent baptism in the name of Christ was obliged to say: 'Lord, I believe; help Thou my unbelief.' (*Mark* IX, 24).

The miracles attributed to Jesus are often, like Isaiah's miracle of the sundial, not supernatural feats, but either simple examples of faith-healing or symbolic acts mistaken as supernatural by Gospel readers. For example, the turning of water into wine at the Galilean marriage feast (*John* II, 1–11) was a mere metaphor. When the guests had drunk so much that the wine supply ran out, Jesus who, as the Messiah was forbidden to taste it (*Proverbs* XXXI, 3–5), made the guests drink water as if it were wine. To show respect for Jesus's austerity, the Master of Ceremonies had the courtesy to say: 'This is the best wine we have had set before us today', meaning that, though wine was a symbol of passionate love (as in the *Song of Solomon*), sexual abstention was better than sexual over-indulgence. The act of love among the Jewish mystics was reserved for the sole purpose of procreation, to fulfil God's commandment in *Genesis* I, 28 'Be fruitful and multiply'.

Many of Jesus's other symbolic acts, such as the so-called 'Feeding of the Five Thousand', were converted into miracles by Christians ignorant of their real meaning. This was perhaps in emulation of those attributed to Apollonius of Tyana, who visited India some twenty years later and there learned yoga and the arts of hypnotic illusion. Jesus's 'miracle' of feeding seems in reality to have been a dramatic demonstration of a calendar mystery, the crowd being invited to take part in the drama. It was based on the identification of manna with bread from Heaven; the bread which the disciples distributed had only symbolic value. The baskets left over contained no more than the fragments already dealt out which, having been dedicated to God, could not thereafter be eaten except by priests. The crowd was nourished, as it were, by heavenly manna.

The miracle of the widow's son raised from the dead at Nain (*Luke* VII, 11) seems to have crept into the Gospels by mistake. To the text 'He went into a city called Nain', the copyist probably added a note 'formerly Shunem, a hamlet of Zarephath, where a widow's son was raised from the dead'. This note will have been taken as referring to Jesus, not to Elisha with whose miracle (II *Kings* IV, 18–37) he is thereupon credited. Apollonius of Tyana was also said—in Philostratus's account of his life commissioned by Septimius Severus's wife Julia Domna to embarrass the Christians—to have raised a widow's son.

To be accepted into the original Jewish Church of Jerusalem headed by James 'the brother of our Lord', a Temple priest who seems to have been a brother of Jesus's adoptive mother, implied a conversion to Judaism and perfect obedience to the Ritual Law. After James's martyrdom in his Temple, this Church survived the massacre at Jerusalem only by a breach both with the Sadducee priesthood and with the militant Pharisees who followed Rabbi Akiba, and by a flight to Pella beyond the Jordan. Later, however, the Jewish Church was repudiated by the Gentile Church, scorned by the defeated Jews and persecuted by the Romans; it had disappeared by the end of the fourth century. There remained numerous Gentile churches founded or sanctioned by Peter, Barnabas, Paul and others in Italy and the eastern Mediterranean, and by St. Thomas in India. Most converts seem to have been recruited from the so-called 'God-fearers': mostly Greek-speaking non-Jews who in the early first century A.D. had abjured the Olympian religion and adopted the Jewish doctrine of a single Almighty God. Although unwilling to 'shoulder the full burden of the Law', they accepted the Ten Commandments and thus earned preferential treatment by the powerful international Jewish merchants and bankers. To go any further in the Jewish faith would have meant consenting to circumcision, which in Roman Law counted as a mutilation that disqualified a man from high public office. It would also have debarred him from convivial meals at the houses of his Gentile friends where the food, however tasty, was ritually unclean. God-fearers had thus become easy converts to Christianity, which by the Apostolic Conference in A.D. 50 freed them from ritual observation of the Law.

Jesus's plain statement in *Matthew* V, 18, that the Law would remain unaltered until the end of the world was qualified by a suggestion that the end of the world preached by John the Baptist was imminent. The Gentile Christians now concluded that their belief in Jesus as Redeemer of the world entitled them to reject the Ritual Law of the unredeemed Jewish nation—on the ground that the Jews had not risen in arms to rescue Jesus from the Cross. When, after Bar Kochbar's unsuccessful revolt in A.D. 132, the rebuilt Temple was dedicated to the Roman God Jupiter, and no Jews were thereafter allowed in the city, the Gentile Christians had won their point: namely that with Jesus's birth the Old Testament had become out of date. The Jews had clearly been rejected by God because the profanation of the Temple, which He had permitted, made it impossible for them to keep this Ritual Law with the necessary sacrifices and other rites performable only there. And, according to Josephus, a Voice had been heard from the Holy of Holies before the destruction of the Temple saying: 'Arise, let us go hence!'. The Christians (*Acts* VI, 14) could now consider themselves His chosen people. This view is first clearly expressed in the late first century *Book of Esdras*, which forms part of the Roman Catholic Apocrypha to the Bible. To emphasize publicly their rejection of the Mosaic Law, the Christian churches changed the Sabbath, the Jewish day of rest, from Saturday to Sunday. They did this ostensibly in honour of his Resurrection, since Jesus was the prophesied Son of Righteousness (*Malachi* IV, 2).

It would have greatly helped the Gentile Christians at this point had they dared to discard the Old Testament, a wholly Jewish document. But Jesus's teachings were largely based on quotations from it—the few exceptions being quotations from later Apocryphal books, not an accepted part of the Biblical canon—and his claim to Messiahship rested on Old Testament prophecies. Moreover, it was on the concept of human and divine love, first preached by the prophet Isaiah and adopted by Jesus, that Christianity rested. Even the command, 'Thou shalt love thy neighbour as thyself', which many Christians suppose to have been Jesus's original saying, is quoted from *Leviticus* (XIX, 18). Jesus's early contemporary, Hillel, the liberal-minded Pharisee teacher and President of the Sanhedrin, held this to be a more pressing commandment than: 'Thou shalt love the Lord thy God with all thine heart, and with all thy soul, and with all thy might' (*Deuteronomy* VI, 4)—because until a man so loved his neighbour he could not possibly love God. Jesus seems to have quoted this saying in the original of *Matthew* XXII, 37–40). The Christian message at its best and purest was summarized in the *First Epistle of John* IV, 8–12. 'He that loveth not knoweth not God; for God is Love. If we love one another, God dwelleth in us.' This is supplemented in *John* XV, 13, with: 'Greater love hath no man than this, that a man lay down his life for his friends.'

The four Gospels, based on Syrian-Greek lecture notes from the original disciples' preaching and edited by

Paul or his Gentile converts, had hardened into something like their present form by the end of the second century A.D. The first three—*Matthew*, *Mark* and *Luke* —called the 'Synoptic Gospels', because Jesus's life is seen as it were from the same point of view in all of them, are followed by *John*. *John* is a more rhetorical and more severely edited gospel but contains some very primitive material. Several other gospels, most of which survive only in quotation, were suppressed by succeeding Church Councils as not wholly suitable for Christian reading. These include the *Protoevangelium*, or 'The Original Gospel of James', which contains some historically important passages: for example, the Virgin Mary is described as a twelve-year-old girl employed in spinning wool for the Temple Sanctuary curtain at the time when she was told by a messenger—John the Baptist?—that she was to become Jesus's adoptive mother, Jesus being then thirty years of age (*Luke* III, 23). Jesus was thus no longer obliged to pay his original Davidic mother the honour that he had once owed her under the Third Commandment, as appears on the occasion when she and her other sons tried to interrupt his preaching (*Mark* III, 32).

It is commonly said that God wrote the Bible: meaning that its many authors all wrote under His inspiration. This claim covers frequent editorial changes in both the Old and New Testaments. The Jewish religion into which Jesus was born had developed down the centuries, and its records were often severely edited. Some two centuries before Jesus's ministry it was reformed by a Pharisee council, after the successful popular revolt led by the Levite Maccabee family against Seleucus, a descendant of one of Alexander the Great's generals. An earlier Seleucid King, Antiochus Epiphanes, had desecrated the Temple Sanctuary, and a collaborationist priesthood in Judaea had crucified Jews for their faithfulness to the true religion: apparently the occasion which gave rise to *Psalm* XXII (My God, my God, why hast thou forsaken me?) quoted by Jesus from the Cross, and piously attributed to King David. This true religion had, however, been a novelty forced on King Josiah of Judah some four centuries previously by an ascetic guild of Hebrew prophets. They appear to have derived their belief in a single Almighty Sun-god from the revolutionary Pharaoh Akhenaton of Egypt. The Jewish King Solomon, who ruled in Israel about the year 1000 B.C. and had close trading connections with the goddess-worshipping Phoenicians, built a huge temple complex at Jerusalem. Its real nature is disguised in the *Book of Kings* where (I *Kings* XI, 4–6) he is said to have been led astray in his old age by foreign wives. From the historian Lucian's description of the first century A.D. temple of the Great Goddess at Hierapolis—meaning Harran, the patriarch Abraham's birthplace—which has the same architectural features as Solomon's, we can judge what sort of ritual was used at Jerusalem. The 'house of the forest of Lebanon' (I *Kings* VII, 2) will have been the Great Goddess's temple; the House of Pharaoh's daughter, whom Solomon is said to have married, but who is not elsewhere mentioned (I *Kings*, VII, 8) will have been the shrine of Ashera, a mysterious divinity, apparently a goddess of wisdom, also worshipped at Hierapolis. The 'House of the Lord' (I *Kings* VI, 1) will have been sacred to Adonis (*Adonai* means 'Lord'), otherwise known as Tammuz, for whose death the women used to mourn annually at the Wailing Wall (*Ezekiel* VIII, 4). This temple was only about a third the size of the Great Goddess's. Solomon's own house (I *Kings* VII, 1) which he took thirteen years to build, is likely to have also been the Temple of the Northern Thunder-god El, whose representative he was.

The Temple rites, as we read in I *Kings* XV, 12, and

II *Kings* XXIII, 7, included ritual prostitution by women and by transvestite men called 'kelebites' (dogs); similar features are recorded by Lucian in the Goddess's temple at Harran. But in King Josiah's reign a book of prohibitions against these elder forms of worship was published as the Fifth Book of Moses and named *Deuteronomy* ('The Second Law'): e.g. *Deuteronomy* XXIII, 17, 18. Josiah forbade the worship of the two goddesses and of Tammuz, and took the seven-fold candlestick as symbol of the universal god El, who now reigned alone. Much of the old ritual remained, however, and was given new interpretations. For instance, the two olive-wood angels placed over the Mercy Seat in the Sanctuary and joined in a close sexual embrace were now interpreted as representing God's conjugal love for his chosen bride, the People of Israel. The corners of the wheat-field had always been left unreaped, the wheat there being dedicated to Tammuz as the spirit of the cornfield; and olives left unplucked at the top of the olive tree were sacred to some other god. Both these gleanings were now allocated to the fatherless and the widowed (*Leviticus* XIX, 9–10). Much the same adaptations of ancient religious festivals were made by the Christians in every European country.

Paul was the chief architect of Christianity, though officially ranking below Peter, with whom he now shares a Saint's Day. Paul's story, as given in the *Acts of the Apostles*, makes confused sense. Had he been born a Roman citizen, as claimed (*Acts* XXII, 27–8), he could not have been so often publicly beaten (II *Corinthians* XI, 24–5), nor could he have faced wild beasts in the amphitheatre of Ephesus unless found guilty of incest or parricide (I *Corinthians* XV, 32). On the other hand, if he had been merely a poor Jewish tent-maker from Tarsus (*Acts* XXI, 39) he could scarcely have afforded the very large sum required for buying a Roman citizenship unless he had used some of the money collected from God-fearers in Asia Minor on behalf of the Jewish Church at Jerusalem (II *Corinthians* IX).

Paul confessed that he was all things to all men: a Jew among Jews, a Gentile among Gentiles (I *Corinthians* IX, 19–20). According to *The Nazarene Gospel*, an early document of the Jewish church, he was a Jew on neither side of his family, but a Greek. His claim to have sat at the feet of Gamaliel, the learned President of the San-hedrin (*Acts* XXII, 3) seems to have been a figure of speech, because when Paul quotes the Scriptures he always quotes the Septuagint translation even when this varies from the Hebrew text insisted upon by Gamaliel and all his fellow-Pharisees. Paul's claim to have once risen to the third of seven Heavens (II *Corinthians* XII, 1–4) shows that he was acquainted with the pre-Christian Alexandrian Gnostics who invented this con-cept and whose influence on the *Gospel according to Saint John* is well known. These Gnostics practised an Oriental way of thought that had come to Egypt, perhaps from China by way of Persia, shortly before the birth of Jesus. Theirs was a philosophy rather than a religion. Some of them became attracted by Christianity and took over the doctrine of Redemption through Jesus as the Messiah, though not the full Christian doctrine. They attacked the Gospels for their historical unreliability, their claims to divine authority and their doctrine of free spiritual equality for all men. The Gnostics pointed out, correctly enough, that few men seemed capable of mystical thought whatever their education.

That Paul was an agent of the pro-Roman Sadducees, who accepted the Law but rejected the Prophets and therefore the Messianic ideal, is proved by his being sent to Damascus with letters from the Sadducee High Priest about A.D. 35 after it had been given by the

Emperor Caligula to Herod Antipas's enemy, King Aretas of Arabia, and ceased to be part of the Roman Empire. These letters can only have been public authorizations for him to collect in Damascus the half-shekel Temple Tax annually due from all Jews throughout the world. In fact, however, as Jesus is said to have told him on the road, he was being sent to persecute the Messiah and his followers. After recovering from his *amauro-blepsosis* or hysterical blindness, and being rescued from the Arabian authorities by the New Covenant sect there (*Acts* IX), Paul repented of his evil deeds. These are known to have included his complicity in the murder of the Christian deacon Stephen. Three years later (*Galatians* I, 18) he returned from Damascus to Jerusalem and there assured the disciples James and Peter of his change of heart. After another eleven years he returned with Barnabas. James and Peter had sent him away, he said, to preach to the Gentiles. Since Jesus had preached that more joy is felt in Heaven over the entry of one repentant sinner than over that of ninety-nine righteous believers (*Matthew* XVIII, 13) Paul felt qualified to lead the missionaries as the self-confessed 'Chief of Sinners' (I *Timothy* I, 15). Peter, a simple Galilean fisherman of whom, we are told, Jesus said, 'Upon this rock I will build my Church' (*Matthew* XVI, 18) was also a sinner. He had broken the Seventh Commandment by drawing his sword in an attempt to rescue Jesus from arrest by the Sadducees' Levite guard—he should have left fighting to the angelic powers (*Matthew* XXVI, 53)—and afterwards three times denied any knowledge of Jesus (*Matthew* XXVI, 75). Moreover, on his visit to Antioch he broke the ritual Law, against eating with non-Jews, to which Jesus had bound the disciples, and concealed his fault from James (*Galatians* II, 11–19) the acting Head of the Church. But confession of one's own evil deeds is a formula still often used by Christian missionaries in slums, prisons and moral rearmament centres.

There seems to have been a complete breach between James and Paul at their second meeting in Jerusalem which took place some thirty years before the Destruction of the Temple. James's view of what Paul and his associates Mark, Luke, Apollos, Timothy, Barnabas and the rest were doing will have been in Jesus's own words, 'To take the children's bread and to cast it to dogs' (*Matthew* xv, 26) i.e. communicating a mystical doctrine, intended for God's chosen race alone, to the ritually unclean Gentiles.

The religious condition of pre-Christian Europe needs a short historical summary. Most Europeans, though not all, acknowledged a supreme God, as opposed to such a supreme Goddess as Cybele, *alias* Rhea, who was worshipped in Crete and Thrace and at Ephesus (*Acts* xix, 28) where she was called Artemis ('Diana'); or as Persephone, who was still worshipped at Locri in Southern Italy for another two or three hundred years. Their God was a god of wrath, power, and inscrutable decisions, who demanded constant sacrifices and in whose name all public oaths were sworn. The word 'God', used in English translations of the Hebrew, Greek and Latin Bibles, originally means 'A supreme being to whom sacrifices are due'. It is of Sanskrit origin, which means that it was brought west by Indo-European invaders from Central Asia. That these were nomadic herdsmen is shown by their language: for instance, our word 'daughter' meant 'milkmaid' in Sanskrit. The word 'God' in all Indo-European languages is masculine, and God has always been credited with male thoughts and actions and served by male priests to whom women owe implicit obedience. This was only to be expected because the nomads' herds were led by bulls, or rams, which kept their younger rivals in their place and to which the cows looked for protection. This nomadic God's chief function was to create thunderstorms and so provide the herds with good grazing. Nevertheless male supremacy was not always the rule, especially in the Mediterranean countries, because these were largely agricultural and because woman, as the fertile sex, took charge of all the fruit-collecting and farming while the men were left to hunt and fish. In contrast, the nomads did not cultivate the soil; they had no need. The Supreme Being therefore had for thousands of years been regarded in Mediterranean countries as a goddess, not as a god.

The early Israelites seem to have come from Asia by way of Armenia and Mesopotamia, where they had intermarried with Northern Semitic herdsmen, and in the second millennium B.C. joined the Hittite invasion of Palestine and Egypt. Their god was Solomon's bull-god El; a name which also survives in the Moslem 'Allah'. A main theme of the early Old Testament is the invasion of agricultural queendoms in Palestine by nomad tribes and a consequent struggle for religious domination. The rape of Jacob's daughter Dinah by Shechem (*Genesis* XXXIV, 2) seems to record the Canaanite conquest of a matriarchal Israelite tribe; but other related matriarchal tribes such as the Hagarites (I *Chronicles* V, 10) meaning 'the children of Hagar', escaped to the less fertile southern deserts.

In Europe, to judge from archaeological finds and early Greek myths, matriarchy had been the general rule until the arrival of nomads from the east. The matriarchal system is still active in parts of West Africa, where descent in certain tribes is reckoned from the mother alone. The father goes to live in her home but takes no responsibility for the welfare even of his sons by her. This situation is reflected in the story of Samson, who takes neither of his two wives to his own home, and in God's command (*Genesis* II, 24) that a man shall 'leave his father and his mother and shall cleave unto his wife'. The first Greek, by the way, said to have broken this ancient tradition was Ulysses, who took Penelope, a Spartan princess, away from her home to his kingdom of Ithaca. A typical matriarchal Creation Story of the Middle East tells how the Mother Goddess Bau became a dove and hatched an egg on the banks of the Euphrates, from which came all trees and grasses, birds, reptiles, fish, beasts and finally men. When however the Supreme Deity became identified with male supremacy in thought and action, a new patriarchal Creation Story came into force, the Creation metaphor being taken from the work of male craftsmen—potters, smiths and architects. God was thereafter increasingly worshipped as the careful planner and silent director of the Universe.

Late in the second millennium B.C., the Greeks adopted a compromise religion to satisfy matriarchs and patriarchs alike. Six small states under patriarchal rule sent male representatives to a Divine Council; six other small states, under matriarchal rule, sent female representatives. These royal priests and priestesses, each representing a tribal god or goddess, agreed to acknowledge the joint rule of the Indo-European Thunder-God Zeus ('El' for the Semites) and the mother-goddess Hera, known as the Queen of Heaven, who was of Libyan origin but identified with the Great Goddess of Syria and Palestine. Zeus and Hera were said to be married—though unhappily—and most of the junior gods and goddesses were regarded as their children. This Greek 'Olympian' religion—so called because the gods were supposed to live in a palace at the top of Mount Olympus, the highest peak in Greece and usually capped with clouds—was eventually accepted by most of Europe and half of the Middle East. But, by the time Christianity appeared, the Divine Council of twelve deities no longer represented merely the original city states. Each god and goddess had by now been given charge of a particular department of life, as in modern government ministries. In Jesus's day Zeus and Hera, the Roman Jupiter and Juno, still remained at the head of affairs, though Hera had long been deprived of any power but that of prophecy. Hermes (Mercury) was the god of travellers, heralds, merchants, bankers and thieves; Ares (Mars) was the god of war; Demeter (Ceres) was the goddess of agriculture; Athene (Athena), goddess of wisdom; Poseidon (Neptune) the god of the sea; Hephaestos (Vulcan), god of all mechanical arts; Apollo, god of music, poetry and medicine; Artemis (Diana) of childbirth and hunting; Aphrodite (Venus) of passionate love. But the Divine council was now agreed to consist of seven gods who could outvote the five goddesses, since Hestia (Vesta), goddess of the hearth, had been politely asked to resign her seat in favour of Dionysus (Bacchus), god of religious intoxication. As a result, the position of women in European society slowly weakened—though not so startlingly as in Israel after Josiah's reformation, when El was said to have driven out his two goddesses after bringing a bill of divorcement against them (*Ezekiel* XXIII, *passim*).

Nevertheless, the Olympian religion was not the only important one in Greece. Indeed, almost everyone mocked at it in private—the national poet Homer had first set the example—though using its ritual on solemn political occasions. Homer seems to have been a member of a secret mystery religion which had survived from matriarchal times, with seats at Eleusis (near Athens), at Corinth, on the island of Samothrace and elsewhere. Persephone, goddess of Life in Death, and Demeter, goddess of the barley, assisted by Dionysus, who induced celestial visions, dispensed certain ancient principles of spiritual conduct, the observance of which would guarantee a man's protection throughout his life on

Demeter's Earth, and his eventual passport into Persephone's Paradise. Admission to these rites was strictly limited: all candidates were required to be whole in mind and body, without a criminal record, of native birth, and with no ancestors of slavish origin.

Personal, as opposed to public, morality in Greece depended largely on the examples set by these mystics. They were forbidden under pain of eternal torture from revealing the ritual or the visions granted them. Nevertheless Greek drama came under the charge of Dionysus's priests, and the famous Athenian tragedies, wholly produced and acted by mystics, were demonstrations of how noble men and women should behave in times of difficulty. Almost nothing is known about the women's mysteries and it is only from occasional hints, such as those dropped by mystics converted to Christianity before the eventual suppression of the Eleusinian rites, that we can guess even at the ritual and the moral teaching of the male mysteries. Adepts of these could alone hope for Paradise; all men disqualified from entry by accident of birth or by notoriously bad behaviour were doomed to flit about forever, like bats, in gloomy underground caves. This explains, in part, the enormous attraction of the Christian message. Paul and his associates who baptized converts into the Christian mysteries—their meetings were clandestine and in Rome usually took place in the underground cemeteries called catacombs—accepted candidates of both sexes, all ages and nationalities, and all classes, bond or free. They even showed particular favour towards penitents with criminal antecedents. Christian baptism, drawn from John the Baptist's example, was in fact the social outcast's first and only chance of achieving Paradise after death in compensation for having lived such a miserable life.

The Supreme Deity remained male, and so did the other two persons of the Trinity worshipped by the

Christians: namely Jesus as God's Son and the Holy
Spirit pictured in the form of a dove—though in Hebrew
the Holy Spirit of God known as the 'Shekinah' was
feminine, whereas *spiritus* was masculine in Latin. The
idea of God as a loving Father was a remarkable concept
of the early Hebrew prophets. The father-figure in all
other religions was stern, proud, harsh. The mother
loved her children openly, the father, especially in
Rome, was forbidden to show them any tenderness.
Jesus is reported in the *Gospel according to the Egyptians*
(quoted by St. Clement) as having said, 'I have come to
destroy the Works of the Female', meaning by 'Works'
all that women did while influenced by the Canaanite
Love-and-Death Goddess Ishtar to undermine or thwart
patriarchal rule. Under Christianity therefore the position of European women showed no improvement. None
of them was allowed to choose her own husband, each
was 'given away' by her father or brother; and no wife
could become a Christian saint unless she had first been
widowed, her husband being considered wholly responsible for her religious life. This rule is still upheld by the
Roman Church, though Paul ruled that a husband's
power over his wife's body was no greater than hers over
his (I *Corinthians* VII, 4). He had, however, permitted
women to prophesy (*Acts* XXI, 9) as Zeus had permitted
Hera; and the Quaker-like Montanist sect of the second
century, which made many converts, used women
missionaries on this authority. But no woman was
allowed to open her mouth in church, and the Montanist
practice was later condemned by Church Councils.
Nevertheless, by a paradox, early Christianity owed its
survival to the patronage of rich and influential women.

The Gospels record Jesus's insistence on a life of
poverty and on taking no more thought for the next day
than the ravens did (*Luke* XII, 24). His 'woe to the rich'
speech is given prominence in the first three Gospels;

so also is his observation that a rich man could no more easily enter Heaven, unless he first distributed his wealth to the needy, than a camel could enter the 'Needle's Eye' (a narrow postern in the walls of Jerusalem) unless its overbulging saddlebags were first removed (*Mark* x, 25, etc.). The priestly Sadducees, Jesus's principal opponents, included several millionaires. Since therefore the early Christians were wholly dependent on charity, this text served to draw gifts and bequests from wealthy idealists who hoped for a place in Heaven. Joanna was the wife of Chuza, Finance Minister to Jesus's most powerful opponent, Prince Herod Antipas. She and Susanna (perhaps her sister), with other unnamed women-friends, had borne the expenses of Jesus's three-year missionary journey (*Luke* VIII, 3). The cost of supporting the twelve disciples and their dependants in what was the most heavily taxed province of the Empire can have been no light burden. But a century later, the Christian faith had spread from the poor and ignorant to converts of high income. The Church's first Imperial patroness was St. Helena, the Emperor Constantine's widowed mother, who mitigated their persecutions in the early fourth century and is said to have miraculously rediscovered the True Cross at Golgotha. The Church's original experiment in communism, also practised by the Dead Sea Essenes, the Free Essenes and the New Covenanters of Damascus, was soon forgotten. To give alms remained a virtue, though rich men were no longer expected to give their entire property to the Church (*Matthew* XIX, 21). St. Paul himself travelled on an expense account (II *Corinthians* VIII, 21).

The Gospel authority for this change is found in the Passion narrative, where frequent quotations from the *Book of Zechariah* (IX, 9; XI, 12; XII, 10; XII, 12; XIII, 7) are never attributed to their source, and where one such text is wrongly credited to the prophet Jeremiah. They all refer to Zechariah's Messianic prophecy 'The Worthless Shepherd', in the light of which Jesus's actions, which seemed to contradict his whole previous teaching, are alone understandable. 'The Worthless Shepherd' was one who would deliberately preach untruth and disobedience to God so that his own father and mother would be scandalized and kill him with a sword. All Israel would suddenly realize that he had deliberately sacrificed himself in this way in order to remind them of God's vengeance; they would 'look upon me whom they have pierced' (*Zechariah* XII, 10). The entire nation would repent and the Kingdom of Heaven would dawn. Unfortunately, later Christians did not realize that Jesus was fulfilling this prophecy and acting out what must have been to him a hideously distasteful dramatic part. They even took seriously his order to put no further trust in God's mercy and loving-kindness, but rather to sell one's cloak and buy a sword, and to make careful provision for creature comforts (*Luke* XXII, 35, 36).

Since Paul had made it his principle to be all things to all men it became Church policy, whenever the lives of its members were in danger, to gain their eventual ends by gently yielding to military or political pressure. Its leaders well understood the natural sinfulness of mankind and the patience needed for redeeming it in the name of Jesus. Despite their care, persecutions began early; the first important one was in the reign of Nero who, aware of the Christians' unpopularity but not in the least interested in their religious opinions, made them scapegoats for the burning of a large part of Rome—an act which he is thought to have arranged himself in order to provide space for an enlargement of his Golden House. Thereafter they became a foreign body within the Empire, neither helping nor hindering its political aims, but regarding this world as vanity and fixing their minds on salvation.

In the critical years of the third century, when the Roman frontier was cracking under barbarian pressure, the Christians, though never openly rebellious, tended to regard such enemies of Rome as God's avengers of their wrongs. Christians had long ceased to be wild-eyed ascetic beggars and were now mainly simple craftsmen and small shop-keepers. They had been severely persecuted for their seemingly unpatriotic refusal to worship the Olympian gods, especially in the reigns of Septimius Severus (193–211), Decius (249–251), Valerian (253–258) and Diocletian (284–305). Sometimes they were brutally tortured or thrown to wild beasts, at other times merely punished by the burning of their Scriptures. Valerianus, son of Galienus (258–266), was the first Emperor who found it politic to recognize this generally unpopular sect by the issue of an edict.

Under Constantine they finally reached their goal, which was for Christianity to be recognized as the official religion of the Empire. Constantine's mother, St. Helena, may well have urged him to favour the Christians, but his political reason is more likely to have been an impending campaign against his colleague Maxientius, which culminated in the victory at Adrianople. A number of Christians had, it seems, formed in the Eastern army what communists now call 'cells', replacing the Mithraic ones; the unexpected recognition of their faith, combined with Constantine's reputed dream of the Cross inscribed '*In hoc signo vinces*', encouraged them to fight like heroes. Constantine even agreed to be baptized before he died, and his many crimes, including the murder of his own son Licinius, called for a truly royal repentance. Constantinius, son of Constantine, actually forbade his subjects to offer Olympian gods sacrifices; but it was many centuries before the Christians were powerful

enough to set up an Inquisition and punish by imprison-
ment, tortures and burning all those who disagreed with
Church dogma. Meanwhile the only punishment was a
bishop's refusal to allow convicted sinners to partake of
the Holy Sacrament for a short or a long period, or for
ever, and so deny them hope of salvation.

The early Christians seem to have come together in
brotherly love with great devotion to principle, though
for want of a central authority, such as the disciples had
enjoyed, the various churches disagreed with one another
on numerous points of doctrine (*Matthew* XXIII, 2). But
they needed leaders and, as happened centuries later
with the early Socialist movement in Europe, the
impassioned idealist was seldom called upon to direct the
policy of his group and protect them against flint-
hearted oppressors. Their leaders, the bishops, who had
originally been in charge merely of food, money and
general expenses, tended to be knowledgeable men of
the world—legalists and bureaucrats rather than saints.
Though Jesus had insisted that a knowledge and confession of sin was a matter wholly between a man and
his God (*Luke* XVIII, 13), the power to forgive sins and
therefore to grant the sinner salvation was vested in
these bishops, and 'sin' came to mean merely a defiance
of Church authority. No other religion at the time was
without priests, so it seemed wise formally to recreate
the priesthood which in Jesus's time had been confined
to certain hereditary Levite families. Christian priests
won their title by a laying-on of hands ceremony said
to have been originated by St. Peter, though he was no
priest; it should have been St. James, who was one.
Moreover, a popular need for sacrifices, acknowledged by
Jesus in his devotion to the Ritual Law and in his eating
of the Passover lamb, was now felt. Hence the conversion
of the bread and wine ceremony, apparently by St.
Paul (I *Corinthians* XI, 23–9) into a sacrificial ritual,

although the eating of human flesh and drinking of blood, even symbolically, was abhorrent to the Jewish mind. David even poured out the drink of water brought to him from the well of Bethlehem by his heroic champions, saying, 'Is not this the blood of the men that went in jeopardy of their lives?' (II *Samuel* XXIII, 17). But Jesus was doubtless making play with two prophecies (*Zechariah* XII, 2 and *Isaiah* LI, 17–22) which refer to a cup of drunkenness, the drinking of which would confuse all Jerusalem in the Last Days.

The Protestant revolt was largely a protest of sincere Bible-readers against so large a Romanizing of Jesus's message, one of love and freedom, that it had become wholly transformed by ritual and Imperial tradition. They complained that Church doctrine now admitted the adoration of idols (namely statues of saints and martyrs)—also attributing moral infallibility to the Pope, which even Jesus had rejected for himself (*Mark* X, 18 etc.); and though the Olympian religion had abolished the attributes or ministries of the twelve gods, those had been shared out among saints. This last was a very natural arrangement. Numerous craft guilds and associations in the Graeco-Roman world had come under the protection of one god or another. The Church authorities therefore substituted saints (many of them historically dubious) for gods, and re-dedicated the temples as churches. Although Christians were expected to pray to God alone, saints were now customarily used as intercessors. Thus St. Agatha of Sicily supplanted Hephaestus (or Vulcan) as patroness of the art of craftsmanship in metal; but later St. Eloi was put in special charge of blacksmiths, the most superstitious guild of all. St. Nicholas took over the temples of Poseidon (Neptune) and protected sailors. St. Hubert became the patron of hunters and ousted the goddess Artemis. St. Michael, a former Jewish archangel, became the patron of soldiers, in place of the god Ares (Mars). St. Christopher, who carried the Christ Child over a river, dispossessed Hercules, who had done the same service for the god Dionysus. In a few country shrines sacred to Venus or Artemis the goddess's names remained unchanged, it being explained that they were also the names of early Christian martyrs. St. George took over dragon-slaying from the pagan god Marduk who had killed the sea-serpent Tiamat; and it is only recently that he has been placed by the Vatican on the list of suspect saints who may be worshipped only locally. The Trinity took over at least one temple from the Three Muses. St. Cecilia was given charge of instrumental music, once Apollo's charge. Eventually lists of saints who specialized in particular diseases were published. Thus St. Marcellus cured headaches and St. Denis of France, syphilis. But though, in theory, mere intercessors they soon became immediately responsible for conferring practical benefits —as an Englishman suffering from some injustice or need approaches a Minister of the Crown rather than the Sovereign who, though nominally responsible for government, may know very little about its practical workings.

At first it had been found convenient to grant every church its independence and not bind it in obedience to some central patriarch, though all were encouraged to send fraternal representatives to General Councils. Gradually, however, smaller churches were put under the charge of provincial bishops who became responsible to their metropolitan archbishop. Then national churches were founded, not merely the Greek and the Roman but the Armenian, the Irish, the Russian and so on. Eventually, when the Greek-speaking churches had become separated from the Latin-speaking ones because of a small doctrinal disagreement about the nature of the Trinity, General Church Councils ceased. Throughout the Dark Ages the Patriarch at Constantinople exercised far greater power than the Bishop of Rome, whose title 'The Pope' seems to have been inherited from the priest-hood of Jupiter. The situation, however, changed dramatically when the Moslem Turks captured Con-stantinople. The Pope, now styled the Vicar of Christ and theoretically controlled by a college of cardinals, governed the Christian world of the West no less absolutely than had the early Roman Emperors who were theoretically controlled by the Senate. Temporal kings and princes came under his spiritual control and paid him homage. To disobey his orders would have endangered their thrones.

Women's gradual restoration to moral responsibility and freedom of choice in love—though the priesthood was still withheld from them—came with the romantic Troubadour movement, a product of the Arabo-Persian poetic tradition introduced by the Moslems who had overrun great parts of Italy, Spain, France and Switzer-land. Pure patriarchy had already been undermined by local superstitions—'superstition' means what has sur-vived from early religious belief, rather than what is untrue—and since Sophia, the Greek word for wisdom, was female, God's holy wisdom became identified with the Virgin Mary. The Black Virgins worshipped in Spain and Southern France during the Middle Ages represent Mary as wisdom—the use of 'black' for 'wise' being borrowed by the Crusaders from Saracen usage, the two words in Arabic being almost identical. Worship of the Virgin in this sense has become a mainstay of Catholicism and has been enthusiastically taken up in all countries with early matriarchal histories. Yet the Virgin has never become the Third Person in the Trinity, has never had any priestesses, and only in the last few years has been officially acknowledged to have been taken up like Elijah (II *Kings* II, 11) into Heaven.

Christianity differed from all other world religions in

insisting that its priests should remain unmarried. The Biblical authority is Jesus's widely misunderstood request for his disciples to make themselves eunuchs for his sake— a request taken literally by occasional Christians such as Origen, who unmanned himself for God's greater glory, and certain Rumanian Puritans, though they do so only after the birth of a first child. In ancient Hebrew religious theory a man and a wife became ritually unclean for three days after intercourse; the text quoted being *Exodus* XIX, 15, where Moses, when about to bring down the Tables of the Law from Mount Sinai, warns the Israelites: 'Come not at your wives', and I *Samuel* XXI, 3–5, where David pleads that his soldiers are pure enough to eat the shew-bread reserved for priests because they have abstained from women for a similar period. Jesus believed, as John the Baptist did, that the 'pangs of the Messiah' which heralded the end of this world were imminent. He therefore warned his married disciples—we know that Peter and his brother James were married (I *Corinthians* IX, 5 and *Mark* I, 30)—to abstain from intercourse lest the great Day of the Lord might overtake them in a state of ritual uncleanliness. (Jesus quotes the Davidic story in a passage misunderstood by early editors as permission for his disciples to take and eat corn from a field put under *Corban* protection, which meant that it was dedicated to Temple use.) Peter's marriage was not anulled, but it seems that he afterwards had only sisterly relations with his wife (I *Corinthians* IX, 5); and though Jesus had pointed out that there would be no marriage or giving in marriage in the Kingdom of Heaven, Paul felt entitled to take a member of the Christian sisterhood as his wife and frankly told the Thessalonians (*Thessalonians* V, 3) to behave soberly, because the Day of the Lord was not immediately at hand. Parish priests in the Greek Church, and all Protestant priests since the time of Martin Luther, have been allowed to marry and raise families, but the Roman Church denies its priests the right to more than housekeepers, its policy being to keep women from winning even indirect control of the sacred mysteries.

A problem which has never been squarely faced by Biblical scholars, who as a rule are directly or indirectly dependent upon the Church for their position, is that of Mithraism. Did the Gentile Christians in establishing their new, non-Jewish faith, borrow religious practices and beliefs from this Middle Eastern religion which was gaining a foothold in the Roman Empire at the very same time? The similarities are remarkable. Mithras was not, of course, a human being like Jesus, elevated to Godhead by his worshippers, but a mythical character, the Spirit of the Unconquered Sun. Mithras's day of worship was Sunday, his birth-feast was December 25th, when shepherds were said to have adored him with gifts; his rites, which included a Holy Communion, were celebrated with bell, book and candle as in the Roman Church; his priests insisted on moral control and abstinence and on the blessedness of female virginity. They also preached the doctrine of Heaven and Hell, the mediation of the Divine Word between man and God, the atoning sacrifice, the warfare between good and evil with the eventual triumph of good, the immortality of the soul, the Last Judgement, the Resurrection of the Flesh and the final destruction by fire of the material universe.

The Mithraists, who had gained control of the legions, and who were ready to make peace with the followers of the Olympian religion, all but gained control of the State in the third century. The survival of Christianity was due mainly to three advantages. First, that its hero Mithras was not a historical character, but an impalpable myth; second, that no women were permitted to partake of its Holy Communion; third, and perhaps most important of all, that it had no easily accessible Book, only a secret tradition. Moreover, its feasts, unlike Christian ones, were often accompanied by wild debauch, offensive to the Roman bourgeoisie. Many of the similarities between the two faiths can be accounted for by common Eastern traditions. Others, such as the substitution of Sunday for Saturday and the Nativity legends, seem borrowed, probably by St. Paul, from Mithraism. The Communion rite, which is omitted from all four gospels and introduced into Gentile Christianity apparently on St. Paul's sole authority as a divine revelation from Jesus, seems borrowed from the Mithraic military rite, however uncharacteristic of Jesus's anti-militarism. Yet the original Mithraic elements were bread and water, wine being introduced later, perhaps as a borrowing from Christian practice.

The impact of Christianity on Europe had become the impact of Europe on Christianity. The Bible was a book open to so many alternative readings, interpretations and justification for either superstitious or novel ways of religious behaviour, that the Church was seldom at peace with itself—just as the Roman Empire had seldom been at peace with its neighbours. The strangest spectacle was the outbreak of religious wars: not merely the Crusades, which were an attempt to free the holy sites of Palestine from the Moslem invaders, but fratricidal war—the destruction of a great part of Southern France during the Papal extinction of the Christian Cathar sect—and finally the bitter religious war fought between Catholics and Protestants in Northern Europe. God was said to be Love. He was also said to be a jealous God, and Jesus himself sadly admitted that he had come into the world to bring not peace but a sword. He was referring to the prophesied battle of Armageddon which would precede the dawn of a New World; but his followers were required to stand by and leave the fighting to God's angels. And whereas the Jews had been cautious in accepting religious converts, Christian missionaries quoted the text of Jesus's wedding-feast parable (*Matthew* XXII, 9), which recommended their going out into the highways and by-ways and compelling the guests to attend. Nor did the Church show the same toleration to Moslems as the Moslems were required to show Christians; for though Mohammed had respected Moses and Jesus as his prophetic forerunners, he refused to believe that Jesus had died on the Cross but held that he had recovered from a death-like trance and moved eastward out of danger. It has been recently agreed by Mohammedan theologians at Al Azhar university, Cairo, that the tomb at Srinagar in Kashmir, for many centuries shown as the place where St. Thomas buried him soon after the Destruction of the Temple, may be revered by the faithful as genuine.

The Bible remains at once the most fascinating and most dangerous book ever published, its texts having been converted by St. Paul's deliberate policy into 'all things for all men'. Verses taken out of context from either the Old or the New Testament, both being now given equal respect, could and still can be twisted to support almost any doctrinal view imaginable.

> For all complain
>   That though God wrote it
> He gave the Devil
>   Power to quote it,
> And by quotation
>   Plainly prove
> That God was dead,
>   And so was Love.

5

Poetry and Obscenity

The word 'obscene' from the Latin *obscenus*, which means 'inauspicious' or 'ill-omened', consists of the words *ob* meaning 'against' and *scaene* (from the Greek *scene*) meaning 'a theatrical performance'. It won its secondary meaning of 'depraved' or 'indecent' when plays, originally performed in honour of deities and heroes under the protection of Dionysus, god of the Mysteries, came to include scenes of indecent buffoonery offensive to the gods themselves. Nero was famous for his stage-obscenities which anticipated by eighteen centuries those recently shown in certain London theatres, but claimed them as his divine prerogative. The natural human tradition had always been for lovers to resort for their secret sexual pairing, like wild goats or gazelles, in hidden places, if possible on high wooded hills, where they would not be interrupted; and never to disclose their amatory secrets. This tradition is of course strongly insisted on by the Shulamite bride of Solomon (*Canticles* II, 17; VIII, 14). When public sexual handling of one another by Roman actors—the 'actresses' being boys—became fashionable, this was at first considered anti-religious and therefore unlucky by the old-fashioned public.

The present cult of written obscenity by so-called poets, especially in the United States, is patently anti-religious: the offence being (to use traditional terms) not only against Dionysus the god of divine illumination, Apollo the god of wisdom, Diana the goddess of female chastity and Vesta, the goddess of the home, but also against the Mountain Goddess of Poetic Love called the

63

Muse. Hence, no doubt, the well-studied breach of all metrical and rhythmic convention by modernist poets. The new obscenity is, however, not merely a smart denial of natural tradition. It is, rather, an agonized protest against the inhuman circumstances of life which in most big cities are controlled by pretenders to religion; as when prisoners shout filthy imprecations against the police who have framed them and are beating them up.

Unfortunately, this perverse fashion has spread upwards through the social strata and the wider the breach with poetic tradition and the traditions of natural religion, the more insensate the pornography and the more chaotic the language. Censorship of stage plays and popular films became so relaxed in the past decade that obscenity, as in Nero's reign, came no longer to be regarded as a portent of ill-luck; and at last the Censor grudgingly bowed himself out. Curiously enough, this trend started not in the filthy, crime-ridden ghettos of American industrial cities but in the over-sophisticated and lovingly ingenuous city of Stockholm; as the legalizing of homosexual brothels did in the gentle country of Denmark.

6

Goddesses and Obosoms

> It was John the Baptist, son to Zechariah,
> Who assumed the cloak of God's Archangel
> And mouthpiece, born on Monday, Gabriel,
> And approaching where his cousin Mary span
> Her purple thread, or sewed a golden tassel
> For the curtain of the Temple Sanctuary,
> Hailed her as imminent mother, not as bride—
> Leaving the honest virgin mystified.
>
> Nor would it be a man-child she must bear;
> Foreseen by John as a Messiah sentenced
> To ransom all mankind from shame—
> But a Virgin Goddess cast in her own image
> And bearing the same name.

Poems should explain themselves, as I trust this does; but it seems correct for once to supply a detailed historical commentary beginning with the phenomenon of *obosoms*, the Virgin theme being of immediate religious importance.

*　　　　　*　　　　　*

In certain primitive West African tribes, matrilineal survivals of the Bronze Age, a royal woman who claimed possession by the power of the Supreme Moon-Goddess, could give birth to an *obosom*—a Twi word apparently derived from *bosom*, the moon. A well-informed account of *obosoms* is given by E. Meyerowitz in *The Akan Of Ghana* (Faber & Faber, 1958). An *obosom* was a visible manifestation of the *kra*, or vital force, derived from the moon, and enjoyed a limited part of the Moon-Goddess Nyame's full powers; she was described as a lesser goddess and given a personal name which her people might invoke in prayer. The *obosom* thus gained for herself the love and loyalty of the newly formed clan rather than the awe due to Nyame; and her mother's human love after she had passed the age of child-bearing and become an *oba panyin* (or elder woman) would often be directed by the *obosom* to lead her people towards a new country where water and food would be plentiful. The *obosom* would meanwhile reveal herself as a totem animal, such as an antelope, falcon, leopard or bat, which could be lovingly relied upon to save her people from danger, and which they called 'the beast within oneself'. This provided the *obosom* with a visible disguise and also recognizable qualities of character drawn from animal metaphor: patience and endurance, for instance, from a falcon and unobtrusive vigilance from a bat. Similar religious customs are reported from Central Africa.

While there were still no male gods in ancient Europe, matrilineal clans gradually united into a tribe, and their chosen Queen-mother, who claimed descent from the Moon-goddess, became the Head of State, took all political decisions and commanded the tribal troops in battle. Athene before her alleged rebirth from the head of the immigrant Greek Thunder-god Zeus seems to have been not only a supreme Love-and-Battle Moon-goddess of North African origin but also patroness of all women's crafts. She was named Neith in North Africa, and Anatha in Syria and Palestine. And in Europe too, as among the Akans, unobtrusive clan-*obosoms* offered themselves for prayer and intercession in private matters to all members of the clan, as their own wise and loving mother. Many such former *obosoms* linger in Greek myth as heroic ancestresses.

In the early second millennium B.C. when patriarchal herdsmen from the East gradually conquered the still matriarchal queendoms of Europe and eventually deprived women of all religious and political power, the change in government implied not only a glorification of male conquest but the gradual ousting of women from their ancient control of all arts and crafts hitherto controlled by the goddess; and thus the reign of maternal love drew to a close.

When Christianity at last superseded the fast-decaying Olympian religion, its five principal goddesses were deposed, and a celibate Christian priesthood assumed control of all public morality. Their God, borrowed from the Jews, is still worshipped as an Oriental monarch of the first millennium B.C. whose courtiers spent all their time in praise of his irresistible power and learned from him to treat women as inferior and irrational beings, their natural slaves. It was this originally Babylonian god who, according to *Isaiah* XXVII, 1, killed the all-powerful sea-and-moon goddess Tiamet. Thus every form of female magic has ever since been denounced by Christian priests and missionaries as blasphemous.

The primitive need among the European peasantry and townsfolk for an *obosom*, if not a Great Goddess, grew yearly stronger as their warlike rulers exploited and harassed them in God's name. Local saints proved insufficient as *obosoms*, and the need was at last satisfied by a cult of the Jewish Virgin Mary, whom Christian mystics began, secretly at first, to identify with the spirit of Divine Wisdom. Mary had hitherto been treated as no more than a convenient, if willing, vessel for the birth of the prophesied Messiah; a pure Virgin, purged of all womanly inclinations for the seduction of men. By the Middle Ages she was being publicly worshipped as the Queen of Heaven, and from her issued local *obosoms* named 'Our Lady of' such and such a place. Yet the true account of her religious origin had never been disclosed by the Christian Church.

In *The Nazarene Gospel Restored* (1953), the

Talmudic scholar Joshua Podro and I provided what seems to have been the first explanation of the Virgin birth that made historical sense. We pointed out that among the prophetic books reverenced by the Pharisees, to whose doctrines Jesus demanded complete obedience from his disciples (*Matthew* XXIII, 1–3) was the *Testaments of the Twelve Patriarchs*. This book, written in the Jewish Hellenistic period, made both the Patriarch Judah and the Patriarch Levi claim to be forefathers of the Messiah, the anointed King who should save Israel. In fact, however, members of both tribes had already gained that honour: King David born from the tribe of Judah had liberated Israel from the Philistines and instituted the Jewish monarchy, and the Hasmonean Kings who rebelled successfully in 167 B.C. against their Seleucid conquerors had been Levite priests. The Pharisees, however, doctors of the Law recognized by the Maccabean Queen Alexandra as the authoritative religious rulers of Israel, read these Testaments as prophetic of what was still to come, not of what had already happened.

Under Scriptural rules, the Messiah would be anointed and enthroned by a prophet. Yet the Pharisees, to discourage popular unrest, had by then long abolished the Guild of Prophets and forbidden any religious or political decision to be taken in Israel except by themselves in full conclave. Nevertheless, the last chapter of the last book in the Hebrew canon, namely *Malachi*, prophesied that Elijah would come back in the Last Days and prepare for the Kingdom of Heaven on earth. The Sanhedrin, which consisted in theory of seventy-two members, always therefore kept one seat vacant for Elijah to occupy.

Jesus admitted the identification of John the Baptist with Elijah—though the only example of reincarnation in the Bible and therefore likely to have been merely metaphorical—and when in Passion Week the Captain of the Temple Guard had asked him by what authority he had done certain things, such as entering into the Temple and fulfilling a prophecy by an ejection of the money-changers, he answered: 'I will tell you if you first tell me whether John the Baptist was or was not divinely inspired.' They dared not give him a straight answer, for fear of the pilgrim mob who supported John's claim to be a prophet, and therefore professed ignorance (*Matthew* XXI, 23–7).

Jesus is stated in *Luke* IV to have been of the tribe of Judah and of Davidic descent, and the earliest accounts that survive make Joseph his physical father; yet we know that 'James the brother of our Lord', also described as 'James the son of Alphaeus' and as 'James the Less', was a Levite priest who took charge of the Jewish Church at Jerusalem after the Crucifixion, leaving Peter to preach the gospel outside the bounds of Israel. Since the tribes of Judah and Levi did not intermarry, the explanation for Jesus's double inheritance can only be that he was born of a Davidic mother but afterwards ceremonially reborn from the priestly Levite line to which James belonged. This solution of the problem is supported by Jesus's having worn a Levite seamless garment forbidden to all the other tribes (*John* XIX, 23), by his having failed to honour his original Davidic mother (*Mark* III, 32) despite his own insistence that no jot or tittle of the Law which included 'honour thy father and thy mother' should ever pass away (*Matthew* V, 18). Also by his distinctively Levite aversion to the prescribed payment of the sanctuary tax (*Matthew* XVII, 27).

For readers unfamiliar with the *Testaments of the Twelve Patriarchs*, here are two paragraphs from Chapter I of *The Nazarene Gospel Restored*:

The authority for the coming of such a Priest-king was found in the *Testament of Levi* II, 10–11:

69

'Thou, Levi, shalt proclaim concerning him that shall redeem Israel, and by thee and Judah shall the Lord appear among men.' And again in XVIII, 2–14, a passage of frequent allusion in the Gospels:

'Then shall the Lord raise up a new priest.
And to him all the words of the Lord shall be revealed;
And he shall execute a righteous judgement upon the earth
    for a multitude of days.
And his star shall arise in heaven as of a king,
Lighting up the light of knowledge as the sun the day,
And he shall be magnified in the world.
He shall shine forth as the sun on the earth,
And shall remove all darkness from under heaven,
And there shall be peace in all the earth.
The heavens shall exult in his days,
And the earth shall be glad,
And the clouds shall rejoice,
And the angels of the glory of the presence of the Lord shall
    be glad in him.
The heavens shall be opened,
And from the temple of glory shall come upon him sanctifica-
    tion,
With the Father's voice as from Abraham to Isaac.
And the glory of the Most High shall be uttered over him,
And the spirit of understanding and sanctification shall rest
    upon him.
For he shall give the majesty of the Lord to His sons in truth
    for evermore;
And there shall none succeed him for all generations for
    ever . . .'

It was also prophesied in the *Testament of Levi* VIII, 11–15:

'Levi, thy seed shall be divided into three offices, for a sign of the glory of the Lord that is to come. And the first portion shall be great; yea, greater than it none

shall be. The second shall be in the priesthood. And
the third shall be called by a new name, because a
king shall arise in Judah and shall establish a new
priesthood, after the fashion of the Gentiles. And his
presence is beloved, as a prophet of the Most High,
of the seed of Abraham our father. . . .'

Again, in the *Testament of Judah*, XXI, 1–4, the patriarch Judah says:

'And now, my children, love Levi that ye may abide,
and exalt not yourselves against him, lest ye be
utterly destroyed. For to me the Lord gave the kingdom, and to him the priesthood, and He set the
kingdom beneath the priesthood. To me He gave
earthly things; to him the heavenly things. As the
heaven is higher than the earth, so is the priesthood
of God higher than the earthly kingdom, unless it
falleth away through sin from the Lord and is domi-
nated by the earthly kingdom.'

Judah further prophesied (*Testament of Judah* XXIV,
1–6 and XXV, 3–5, omitting Christian interpolations):

'And a man shall arise, like the sun of righteousness,
Walking with the sons of men in meekness and righteousness;
And no sin shall be found in him.
And the heavens shall be opened unto him,
To pour out the spirit, the blessing of the Holy Father;
And he shall pour out the spirit of grace upon you;
And ye shall be unto Him sons in truth,
And ye shall walk in His commandments first and last.
Then shall the sceptre of my kingdom shine forth;
And from your root shall arise a stem;
And from it shall grow a rod of righteousness to the Gentiles
To judge and to save all that call upon the Lord.'
etc.

71

Jesus's adoption into the Tribe of Levi had clearly been arranged by John the Baptist, who was himself a Levite. The most explicit account of the Annunciation, found in the very early and once canonical *Protoevangelium* (X and XI) presents Mary as a girl who span the thread used in weaving the sacred curtain for the Holy of Holies. Both here and in the Canonical Gospels, John the Baptist assumes the role of the Archangel Gabriel, the Archangel of Monday and therefore of prophetic utterance and announces Mary to be the destined Mother of the Messiah. Yet as a weaver or spinner she must have been still pre-nubile so as not to defile the curtain with her menstrual blood, and the *Protoevangelium* makes her only twelve years old. She is then sent for a while to John's mother, Elizabeth. After Jesus's preliminary ordeals, intended to make him fit for his installation as King (*Matthew* IV), he will have been drawn from under her skirts in a symbolic rebirth, given a new name and anointed as King. Mary afterwards accompanied him in his three-year progress through Judea and Galilee, even to the Cross. This symbolic rebirth of a man as King is a ceremony recorded not only in ancient Greece (Diodorus Siculus IV, 39) but also in modern Central Africa.

Yet the Gospel tradition handed down by the disciples —especially of Jesus's comments on the Scriptures, which they were not permitted by Pharisaic Law to record in writing—has been so defaced by Syro-Greek converts who recorded it, that Jesus's two mothers have been constantly confused, and his adoptive mother further confused with the Galilean Mary Magdalene or 'Mary of Magdala' possibly because she had been herself known as Mary M'gaddla (the weaver).

In the slow progress of Christianity, a hunger for the ancient Mother Goddess eventually spread from the peasants to the upper classes and called for her secret restoration; so that to most Catholics the Virgin Mary is now a far more important source of religious inspiration than her son. We may in fact describe the Blessed Virgin as an *obosom* born to the innocent and bewildered Mary M'gaddla, not against her will but by divine intervention. Catholics in need of spiritual comfort now kneel before the Blessed Mary rather than before the Crucifix of her suffering Son. This is because men and women in real trouble naturally prefer the support of a calm mother to that of a miserably suffering elder brother. Women, indeed, have a natural aversion to spectacles of extreme misery caused by man's injustice to man. Few young women in love, especially if they are carrying or nursing a baby, or tending the sick, wish to expose themselves to this commemorative record of male torture, and therefore to a symbolic denial of their own powerlessness in face of male perversity. If a sensitive woman ponders too painfully on the seven stations of the Cross she risks souring her milk, aborting her child and turning her own wits. Thus the figure of Jesus dying on the Cross in a courageous but mistaken attempt to fulfil certain fanatical Jewish prophecies of the immediate end of the world—not, as the Church claims, to save mankind—revives the original sense of man's cruelty to man and to his womenfolk, and little by little loses spiritual importance.

Historically, therefore, the Virgin represents the will to live, heal and love. Mary, though forced to remain chaste for the rest of her life, is credited with a true sense of love for her adoptive son, and thus a sympathy with all men and women in trouble or danger. The poem about John the Baptist and Mary M'Gaddla, with which this discussion began is, in fact, prophetic of a radical change in the Christian religion. Since the Church has failed to bridge the growing gap between Gospel tradition and the now accepted but incompatible history of first century A.D. Palestine—also between the Gospel scene and modern political, industrial, scientific and moral systems—belief in a prophesied Messiah and a final Day of Judgement has everywhere declined. Professed Christians find themselves lost in a desert of cruelty, confusion, pollution, danger and disaster. They do not wish to confront themselves with that naked suffering figure on the Cross. It is too realistic, and for many brain-washed soldiers and security police returned from Vietnam, too reminiscent of their own Asian victims to be more than a mockery. They must rather rediscover the lost centre of the world: the Mother Goddess, whose task has always been to keep her lands clean, orderly and in peace, to pardon the repentant and to shower blessings on all who love her. And if Mary has failed us, from being a Church puppet too long activated by loveless strings, a new immaculate Goddess must somehow be provided for those still worthy of her.

England, by the Protestant defeat of Catholicism at the Battle of Naseby (1645), lost its title of 'Merrie England' largely because of the consequent ecclesiastical ban on what the Puritans called Mariolatry. Fortunately we have still somehow preserved the tradition that allows Queens to be anointed and to reign as though Kings; and have therefore kept the distinction between Her Majesty's human identity, with all its personal foibles, and her religious identity. Armies have fought to the death for the Queen, whose image on coins remains youthful for many decades after her succession; and there are regiments and corps which count themselves doubly fortunate to be under her titular colonelcy. What is more, the Queen is raised a hands-breadth above the Law, and thus enjoys the right to bestow a free pardon on subjects who seem to have been over-harshly sentenced. Dictatorships and parliamentary republics which deny prisoners any recourse beyond the supreme judiciary, are less to be envied. The Queen in fact gives birth

at her Coronation to an *obosom*, and the national anthem
is the hymn that celebrates the birth. If this *obosom* may
be said to have a totem animal it will naturally be the
horse, which has been the traditional totem animal of
Britain since immemorial times—with lion, eagle and
unicorn as its supporters.

What other *obosoms* have survived into this irreligious
century? And what close-knit clans still preserve a sense
of dedicated loyalty, however riddled they may be with
impostors? I can be sure of only five. There is the physi-
cian clan, founded by Hippocrates; its *obosom* is Hygeia
(Health) whose mother was Peitho ('Persuasion') and
who was worshipped at Argos jointly with Asclepius, the
God of Medicine. There is the dancers' clan; its *obosom*
is Terpsichore ('Joy in the Dance') a daughter of the
mountain goddess Musa. Then there is a clan of pure
musicians who still keep faith with their Muse Poly-
hymnia. And another of devoted craftsmen whose
obosom is Aglaia, wife to Hephaestus whose mother conceived him without male intervention. Also the small
and fast diminishing clan of lyric poets whose *obosom* is
Erato ('the lovely one'), a daughter of the same goddess
and also nurse to Dionysus, the God of Inspiration. All
these five clans work, or are expected to work, under
excessive self-discipline.

There remains what is rumoured here and there to be
the most powerful *obosom* of all: it protects an unorgan-
ized and nameless clan existing from time immemorial,
the members of which refer to themselves simply as
'Us', and which has no known origin or history. Its
members, drawn from all races, religions and occupa-
tions, are traditionally confined to the sacred number
4,000, a figure which no increase or decrease in the world
population is said to alter. Four thousand has, it seems,
been chosen metaphorically: it is a multiple of the basic
male number 2, raised to the fifth degree, by the creative

female number 5 raised to the third degree in honour of the moon's three phases. The 'Us' people, who are their own masters and incapable of deception, recognize one another at once without any exchange of secret signs and at once join forces in undertaking any task which their apparently accidental encounter has imposed on them. This *obosom* has no name, because to name is to define, to define is to analyse, and to analyse is to destroy; nor does it possess any particular totem animal, because that would limit the clan's magic capacities.

The Romans at the height of their power perfected the technique of *elicio* which meant to elicit (by bribery, force or trickery) the secret names of gods who ruled neighbouring tribes; then to use these names for enticing them to Rome, where they had been promised new temples under their own priests. So Rome became a jackdaw's nest of spoil, and the border tribes, robbed of divine protection, fell under her greedy control. A nameless *obosom* can never fall victim to *elicio*, nor can it be listed in a religious encyclopedia, but remains religiously, politically and geographically indefinable. Such an *obosom* may well be the sole directive force capable of carrying mankind safely through its present threat of almost universal lovelessness towards some semblance of the prophesied Golden Age. Let Mary continue to be the Queen of Heaven for the general populace, but let the nameless *obosom* which is the unecclesiastical counterpart of what Christians call 'the Holy Spirit' continue to watch over the scattered clan that has become mankind's sole creative but secret conscience.

7

The Universal Paradise

We have narrowed our minds by a neglect of physical senses: relying on reason, we no longer see, hear, taste, smell or feel anything like so acutely as our primitive ancestors did, or as most little children still do before their education hardens. Henry Vaughan's *The Retreat*, imitated by Wordsworth in his better known *Intimations of Immortality*, begins:

> Happy those early days, when I
> Shin'd in my angel-infancy!
> Before I understood this place
> Appointed for my second race,
> Or taught my soul to fancy aught
> But a white celestial thought;
> When yet I had not walked above
> A mile or two from my first love,
> And looking back (at that short space),
> Could see a glimpse of his bright face;
> When on some gilded cloud or flower
> My gazing soul would dwell an hour. . . .

Civilized man notices a gilded cloud and, at best, mutters 'cumulus' or 'cirrus' or 'mare's tail', speculating on the weather it portends; notices a flower and dismisses it with a casual recognition of variety. To gaze at a wild rose or buttercup for even a minute and find illumination in the sight, would never occur to him; if only because all his senses are blunted by a persistent disregard of the ugly smells, ugly sounds, ugly sights and unpalatable tastes which the struggle for existence entails. His spirit, also, has lost touch with the ideas of mystery,

grace and love that originally informed it: intellect and
habit starve out imagination. How to awaken these
dormant capacities is a problem seldom raised, except by
mystics, who usually suggest a daunting formula of
spiritual exercises, designed to tame bodily lusts. Some
claim to have themselves visited Paradise in a state of
trance so induced, and to have found it the seat of true
felicity and perfect wisdom. Here is a typical passage
from Thomas Traherne's *Centuries of Meditation* (he
was a contemporary of Vaughan's):

> The corn was orient and immortal wheat, which
> never should be reaped nor ever was sown. I thought
> it had stood from everlasting to everlasting. The dust
> and stones of the street were as precious gold: the
> gates were at first the end of the world. The green
> trees when I first saw them through one of the gates
> transported and ravished me: their sweetness and
> unusual beauty made my heart to leap, and almost
> mad with ecstasy they were such strange and beautiful
> things . . . all things abided eternally as they were
> in their proper places. Eternity was manifest in the
> light of the day and something infinite behind every-
> thing appeared, which talked with my expectation
> and moved my desire.

Today, the main alleviations for the stress of commercial and industrial life are organized religion,
organized entertainment, drink. Organized religion may
sober the spirit, but except among the more ecstatic sects,
rarely purges it. Organized entertainment distracts, but
does not illuminate the mind. Though some poems,
melodies, works of art, love-affairs and fever dreams may
give glimpses of a lost magical reality, their spell is short-
lasting: it does not create such a permanent nostalgia
for the fairyland of childhood as possessed, say, John

Clare in Northampton asylum. The hard, dirty, loveless, synthetic world reasserts itself as the sole factual truth. Yet a superstititious dream that, somehow, happiness, love, glory, magic lie hidden close at hand, protects the world from the nervous breakdown of which recent wars have been symptomatic: a dream that, when fostered by films and family magazines, becomes optimistically attached to personal success in a career or marriage and, when fostered by the churches, to a Paradisal afterworld.

In ancient times, 'Paradise' was strictly reserved for an illuminated aristocracy, until the Church at last threw open the gates to all, however brutish or feeble-minded, who would accept baptism. Priests then preached Heaven's glories (attainable only by a belief in Christ) as the reward of patience and humility after traversing this vale of tears. But St. John's Apocalyptic Paradise is borrowed from chapters of the pre-Christian *Book of Enoch* which are themselves based on the 'Eden' chapters of *Ezekiel* and *Genesis*; and these, again, on the Babylonian Paradise described in the Gilgamesh Epic and elsewhere. The Persians knew a similar Paradise; and their name for it, *paridaeza*, yields the Syrian-Greek word *paradeisos* and the Hebrew *pardess*. Those middle-Eastern Paradises, so far back as the Sumerians, are reported as delightful mountain-top gardens watered by a four-headed crystal river, their fruit-trees laden with flashing jewels; and a wise serpent always haunts them. Rare humans who enter Paradise while in a state of grace are granted 'perfect wisdom' by the Serpent— 'knowledge of good and evil' means knowledge of 'all things that exist'—and only the herb of immortality is denied them. Thus Gilgamesh, having visited the jewelled Babylonian Paradise, dived to the sea-bottom and drew up a herb of immortality; but the Serpent took it from him, and he meekly resigned himself to death.

Adam and Eve were driven out of Eden ('pleasure') by God lest they might discover and eat the fruit of immortality; the Cherub, on guard at the gate thereafter with a flaming sword, is the very Serpent who gave them the fruit of knowledge. The King of Tyre, though perfect in beauty and wisdom, is figuratively expelled from Eden (*Ezekiel* XXVIII) for claiming to be an immortal god with a seat in the heart of the sea. *Enoch* mentions both the tree of wisdom and the tree of life; and *The Secrets of Enoch* places the latter in the Third Heaven, a paradise to which St. Paul claimed to have been caught up.

Greek mythographers told of a Paradise on Mount Atlas, the 'Garden of the Hesperides', guarded by a hundred-headed Serpent; but made Heracles shoot the Serpent, take away some of the jewelled fruit, and become immortal. This Paradise, like the Sumerian one that antedates Gilgamesh's 'Garden of Delights', belonged to a Mother-goddess—it was Hera's before she married Zeus—not to a male god. Christians chose to identify the Serpent in Eden with Satan; they preached that Jesus Christ, a 'Second Adam', lives permanently in Paradise, having expelled the Serpent, and is ready there to welcome all believers when the Serpent has finally been destroyed on the Day of Judgement.

Why do paradises follow a traditional pattern, widespread and persistent enough to be shared even by Polynesians and pre-Columbian Mexicans? The evidence suggests that, originally, a common hallucinogenic drug causes the paradisal visions and provides the remarkable mental illumination described as 'perfect wisdom'. One such drug was certainly used in Central America before the Spanish conquest. Professor Roger Heim and R. G. Wasson's massive work, *Les Champignons Hallucigènes de Mexique* (Paris, 1958), contains a coloured reproduction of a fresco from the Aztec city of Tepantitla, dated between 300 and 600 A.D., which

shows a soul visiting Paradise. The usual elements are
there: a river (stocked with fish), bordered with flowers
and bejewelled trees, haunted by bright coloured butter-
flies and a spectacular serpent. The soul stands open-
mouthed, weeping tears of joy and wonder, his body
connected to the river by a blue thread. This river is
shaped like a mushroom and, at its source—the centre
of the mushroom head—lurks Tlalóc, God of Mysteries,
in toad form, the water issuing from his mouth. Tlalóc,
who often wore a serpent head-dress, was also a god of
lightning. He used a sea-shell as another emblem, and
'had his seat in the midst of the seas': at the bottom of
the fresco an underwater grotto appears, marked with a
cross, the four heads of which are mushrooms. Since
Wasson had been admitted to the very rite thus pictured,
he found little difficulty in deciphering the symbolism.

His ritual experience came as the culmination of a
study on which he and his wife had been engaged for
years: that of mycophobia. Mycophobia, the unreasoning
fear of mushrooms, affects whole populations in Europe,
Asia and Africa, being total in some regions, in others
modified by certain exceptions (such as the white field-
mushrooms among the English), elsewhere non-existent.
Now, a few mushrooms, easily distinguished from
edible varieties, do contain a mortal poison; but most are
palatable, if not delicious. Why, the Wassons asked,
when wholesome fruit and vegetables are eaten freely,
with a disregard for the poisonous or the inedible, should
this selectivity be denied the mushroom? Why should
horrible and obscene names be applied to edible mushrooms? Perhaps mycophobia pointed to an ancient
taboo, like that which has given Jews and Moslems a
disgust of pork and Northern Europeans a disgust of
horse-flesh—nutritious and tasty meat—both pig and
horse having once been holy animals. And, since mushrooms figured alongside toads, snakes and devils in

81

numerous late mediaeval paintings, and still bear popular names connected with toads, snakes and devils, it looked as if they might have been sacred food in a pagan rite, preserved by the witches of Western Europe who kept toads and snakes as diabolic 'familiars'.

A particular variety of mushroom, the *amanita muscaria*, in Britain called 'fly-cap', grows under birch-trees in Northern countries, where it is scarlet with white spots; but under conifers to the southward. Fly-cap induces in the Korjaks, a Palaeo-Siberian tribe of Kanchatka, a boisterous ecstasy which helps them to consult ancestral spirits and utter prophecies. The Wassons guessed that the mushroom had been similarly used in Europe but reserved for the priesthood; that for security reasons the taboo had been extended to cover all mush-rooms on pain of death; and that this taboo hung on long after the rites came to an end—except in countries where famine forced the common people to defy it and they became positive mycophiles, as all Slavonic peasants now are. The name 'toadstool', particularly applied to fly-cap, is apt; because it contains a poison, *bufonenin*, which also is exuded by toads from their 'warts' when frightened.

Moreover, early Spanish archives mentioned Mexican mushroom oracles that, though officially extinct, were still rumoured to operate in secret far from civilization. A certain mushroom was known as 'God's body' by the Mazateks of Oaxaca Province, because sacramentally eaten. The Wassons, learning of this, visited Oaxaca during the June mushroom season, and were able to attend an oracular meeting at which the *curandero* (healer) who took charge ceremoniously ate certain small ill-tasting mushrooms and, speaking for the god, gave an unexpected, surprising and accurate answer to the question they had asked him. Later when invited by a *curandera* to eat the mushrooms themselves, they understood the solemn local tradition about the feast: 'One knows all; one even sees where God dwells.' Their visions recalled the heaven shown on the Tepantitla fresco, and it became clear that they had been symbolically eating the body not of Christ, but of the god Tlalóc.

Wasson has since investigated other regions where the cult survives, and found religious rules common to all. Devotees, before partaking in a mushroom feast, must fast, abstain from sexual intercourse, and be at peace with the world and themselves. Whoever disregards these rules (the *curanderos* and *curanderas* agreed) may see such demonic visions as to wish they had never been born. Christian, Jewish, Greek and Babylonian Heavens, it should be recalled, have a Hell which complements Paradise; and the usual vision is of innumerable demon faces grinning from lurid caverns. But those who attend such a feast while in a state of grace, report that the mushrooms not only sharpen their intelligence, so that they seem to possess 'perfect wisdom', but shower on them what Christians call 'the peace and love that passes all understanding'—a strong, non-erotic sense of spiritual comradeship.

The Roman Catholic Church teaches that Paradise cannot be attained except by repentance; and prepares every sinner for the journey with the *viaticum*, a symbolic consumption of Jesus Christ's body and blood, after asking him to purge his soul by a sincere confession. From what religion, it should be asked, did St. Paul borrow this rite, since it is not attested in the Gospels and is an infringement of the Hebrew law against the drinking of blood? A question that leads to another: in what pre-Christian cult did any god deliver oracles when his flesh was symbolically eaten—as the Mazateks now believe that Tlalóc-Christ does? Tlalóc, we know, was the spirit of the lightning-engendered toadstool. Further questions arise. What European god claimed this nativity? Or had mystical associations with the serpent or the toad? Or possessed a submarine retreat? Or assisted at mysteries where ineffable visions were witnessed?

The sole European deity known to have matched Tlalóc in these respects was Dionysus. Born as a serpent-crowned child from the Earth-goddess Semele, whom a flash of lightning had impregnated, he went through a variety of transformations, was then torn to shreds and eaten by the Titans, but restored to life by his grand-mother, the goddess Rhea, Creatrix of the world; possessed a submarine retreat in the grottoes of the Sea-goddess Thetis; and assisted at the chief Greek Mysteries, under the protection of goddesses.

The Greek poets tell how when Dionysus' maenads tore off Orpheus' head, it continued to prophesy. The head of Pentheus, another figure in the Dionysus myth, was torn off by his own mother Agave; both incidents could refer to the practice of tearing the mushroom head from its stalk—heads alone are used at Mexican oracles. The Eleusinian Mysteries, sacred to the Goddesses Demeter and Persephone, and also to Dionysus, were preceded by fasting and a ritual bathe in the sea, where devotees transferred their sins to scape-pigs. They then entered a temple, drank mint-water and ate pastries baked in magical shapes and carried in baskets. As a result, they saw celestial visions which could never afterwards be forgotten. The meaning of the Greek word *mysterion* ('mystery') is disputed, but since the mysteries were an autumnal festival complementary to the Spring *anthesterion*; and since this means 'flower-springing', *mysterion* may well mean *myko-sterion*, or 'mushroom-springing'.

A distinction should here be drawn between the wild Dionysian orgies of Maenads who went raging over the hills, often in the company of Satyrs (a pre-Hellenic mountain tribe), and the decently conducted temple-mysteries, where no violence occurred. Pliny's remark that an awed hush 'descends on people if a toad is placed among them' suggests that Dionysus, like Tlalóc, had a toad epiphany. But the celestial visions at the mysteries are unlikely to have been produced by fly-cap, which loses its toxic quality when cooked, and could not well be introduced raw into food and drink. However, the toxic qualities of *panaeolus papilionaceus*, a hallucinogenic toadstool shown on an early Greek vase and now known to have figured in the European witch cult, resist cooking; its liquor may have been mixed in the mint-water, and its flesh baked in the magical pastries. I believe, but cannot prove, that fly-cap, which appears on a carved Etruscan mirror at the feet of the criminal Ixion, was the original mushroom sacred to the universal Toad-god; and that the more tranquil and equally delightful properties of *panaeolus papilionaceus* and *psilocybe*, which do not contain *bufonenin*, were discovered by later experiment and also placed under the Toad-god's charge. Fly-cap grows in both hemispheres, and the mushroom-stones of Guatemala show Tlalóc in toad shape, seated underneath a mushroom which appears to be a fly-cap, not a *psilocybe*.

Some of the Eleusinian pastries had phallic shapes and, indeed, *mykes* ('mushroom') also means 'phallus' in Greek; others like piglings (a widespread term for mushrooms); some may have been shaped like toads and serpents. A common name for the toad in European folklore is 'the cripple', because of his clumsy feet; and 'Dionysus' means 'lame god'. One Greek hero who, according to the myths, at first resisted Dionysus, but presently saw the light, was Perseus, King of Argos and founder of Mycenae. Punished for his obduracy with an outbreak of madness among the Argive women—they began eating their own babies raw, as also happened at Thebes when Pentheus resisted the cult—Perseus dedicated a temple to Dionysus at Mycenae. Argos had a toad as its badge, and Perseus is said to have named Mycenae after a mushroom found on the site, 'from which proceeded a stream of water'. He also made visionary flights through the air, paid a visit to the 'Stygian nymphs' on the slopes of Mount Atlas—presumably the Hesperides, who were later kind to his descendant Heracles—and claimed the same sort of nativity as Dionysus, having been engendered by Zeus in a shower of gold. Phryneus, the Toadstool-Dionysus to which these myths point, lay securely hidden behind the Wine-Dionysus and the Grain-Dionysus. Apart from a menacing Greek proverb 'Mushrooms are the food of the gods' nobody mentioned the subject. Greek peasants are mycophobes.

Baby-eating, a practice not associated with any Greek cult except that of Dionysus, also figured (according to Catholic missionaries) in the Aztec rain-making rites of Tlalóc. This god's name meant 'Pulp of the Earth' (i.e. mushroom), and he lived at Tlalócan, a mountain paradise, with certain Grain-goddesses and his gentle sister-spouse Chalchiuthlicue, patroness of streams and family-life. Some centuries before the Spanish conquest, matriarchy and clan-totemism had been superseded among the Aztecs by patriarchy and individual totemism. Tlalóc thus officially escaped from the tutelage of the goddesses, just as Dionysus did in Classical Greece when he was raised to the Olympic Council of Twelve, and took over the Barley-goddess Demeter's winnowing festival, the Halos. Yet in the Mysteries, Dionysus seems still to have been subservient to her and Persephone. Similarly, the Mazatek *curandera* who initiated the Wassons addressed the Christianized Tlalóc as if he were her wayward son, and she a goddess. It is possible that, alike in Greece and Mexico, the 'babies' eaten in sacred pictures were really mushrooms.

There may have been a mushroom cult in pre-Exilic

Israel. Plutarch later claimed that the identity of Jehovah and Dionysus could be proved; and it is true that the Feast of Unleavened Bread and the Feast of Tabernacles, at both of which wine was drunk, closely resembled the rites of Tammuz-Dionysus. By Plutarch's time, however, Jehovah had long since been exalted into a transcendental God incorporating all the old deities and planetary powers; and his original goddess-companions Anatha and Ashima, corresponding to Demeter and Persephone, were banished from their temples on Mount Zion. The Serpent figured not only in the Garden of Eden story, but as the divine Serpent-image with which Moses allayed a plague, and which Hezekiah, a reforming King of Judah, later destroyed as a 'graven image'. One first-century Jewish sect, the Ophites, worshipped a Serpent-Jehovah.

Though neither toads nor toadstools are mentioned in the Bible, the fantastic story of the three hundred foxes which Samson bound together in pairs, with flaming torches tied to their tails, and let loose among the Philistine cornfields, suggests toadstool intoxication. 'Little foxes' is a widespread name for the edible *chanterelle* mushroom; and 'little foxes with fire in their tails' might well mean the fox-coloured Palestinian fly-cap. That Samson used fly-cap to intoxicate a war-band of three hundred men, and sent them to burn the enemy corn, makes good military sense; a Swedish regiment is said to have once used the same powerful drug during the Napoleonic wars. A reference to the erotic power of these mushrooms occurs in the *Song of Solomon*.

Moreover, the Ark of the Covenant contained golden 'ermrods' described as *ex-voto* objects sent by the Philistines as an atonement for its capture, in vengeance of which they had been stricken by Jehovah with ermrods ('haemorrhoids')—curiously enough, the very punishment inflicted by Dionysus on the Athenians who

87

despised his worship. Since ex-voto objects never represent a disease or deformity, but always a limb or organ when restored to health, these ermrods must have meant something else—perhaps the heads of mushrooms as vestiges of a suppressed oracular cult. 'Boils' and 'piles' are common folk-names for mushrooms.

The Christian sacrament of bread and wine was a love-feast in Hellenistic style. Initiates of the Lesser Eleusinian Mysteries, who had to undergo a period of probation before being admitted to the Greater Mysteries, saw no celestial visions. Presumably, the mystagogues withheld the sacred hallucinogenic agent until sure of a candidate's worthiness; he received bread and wine only, symbols of the Grain-Dionysus and the Wine-Dionysus. The Church has indeed banished the Serpent from Paradise. Her sacramental elements give the communicant no visionary foretaste of the new Jerusalem. The disappointment often felt by Protestant adolescents at their first communion is a natural one—the priest promises more than they are able to experience.

Granted, many Christian mystics and Jewish mystics have undoubtedly seen Paradisal sights, but always after a life of intense spiritual struggle; and these often alternate with terrifying visions of Hell. It is now therefore usual to treat mystics as schizophrenics, arresting them and prescribing electric shock treatment if their enthusiasm has caused a breach of the peace. The Church herself is apt to discourage a mystic who claims to have seen sights denied to his ecclesiastic superiors; suspecting him, at best, of spiritual pride. This type of schizophrenia is chronic, uncontrollable, and what is called 'anti-social'. Only when mystics have written poems or painted pictures, in which the illumination cannot be denied, and only when they have been dead for some years— for example St. John of the Cross, El Greco, Blake, van Gogh—are they likely to be valued as great souls.

The use of hallucinogenic mushrooms, on the other hand, induces a temporary, controllable schizophrenia within the Mazatek social scheme, and the sole religious demand on participants is that they shall enter the circle fasting, with a clear conscience and a quiet mind. When I ate *psilocybe* in January 1965, among friends, a recording of the *curandera's* invocation to Tlalóc as Christ gave the rite a decent solemnity. *Psilocybe* must be eaten in complete darkness—because the least light, even strained through the eyelids, becomes painful as soon as the drug takes effect. The visions last for some four and a half hours. According to the Mazateks, a novice seldom sees persons or historical scenes: he finds it enough to enter the 'Garden of Delights'. The second and third feast may widen his experiences. Adepts learn to direct their minds wherever they please, visit the past, foretell the future. As a novice, I was satisfied with a view of Paradise, which I reached by a preliminary descent to the blue-green grottoes of the sea, and a passage through blazing treasuries of jewels. In this mountain-top Eden, the musical notes of the *curandera's* song could be *watched*, as they slowly fell and turned into leaves, flowers, or twisted golden chains. . . . Fields of Traherne's 'orient and eternal wheat' were also visible at the mountain-foot, as I looked down. A sense of utter peace and profound wisdom held me, until the influence began to fade and I rose up refreshed. I now understand why the Buddha, on his deathbed, is said to have joined his disciples in a feast of 'piglings': if these were mushrooms, they will have taken him straight to the Indian Paradise.

Civilized consciences revolt against the abuse of hallucinogenic drugs—most of them habit-forming, dangerous and unobtainable except by prescription or in the black market. Spirits, tobacco, tranquillizers—all harmful if habitually taken—are however on unrestricted sale and, because they provide no visions (apart from the fearful hell of *delirium tremens*), the Churches condone their use; for hard liquor merely depresses the senses, tobacco and tranquillizers merely dull them.

Psilocybin, the active principle of *psilocybe*, has recently been isolated, and is synthetically made in Switzerland. At present, the medical profession controls the supply, and uses it for the diagnosis of mental illness. But, since the formula has been published, even severe legislation will not prevent the general public from access to the product. It seems likely, therefore, that what was for thousands of years a sacred and secret element, entrusted only to persons chosen for their good conduct and integrity, will now be snatched at by jaded sensation-seekers.

*   *   *

They will be disappointed. The word 'drug', originally applied to all ingredients used in chemistry, pharmacy, dyeing and so on, has acquired a particular connotation in modern English, which cannot apply to *psilocybin*: 'to drug' is to stupefy, rather than to quicken, the senses. *Psilocybin* provides no welcome semi-death in drunken stupor: though the body is relaxed, the mind is conscious throughout, indeed, supra-conscious. Psychiatrists at the Lexington Addiction Centre, Kentucky, who give *psilocybin* to alcoholics as a means of discovering why they are trying to escape from reality by drink, find that it intensifies and lays bare mental conflict. Experimentalists are therefore likely to see visions evoked by their own uneasy consciences: weeping for grief, not joy; or even shuddering aghast.

Good and evil alternate in most people's hearts. Few are habitually at peace with themselves; and whoever prepares to eat hallucinogenic mushrooms should take as careful stock of his mental and moral well-being as initiates took before attending the Eleusinian Mysteries. This peculiar virtue of *psilocybin*, the power to enhance personal reality, turns 'Know thyself!' into a practical precept; and may commend it as the sacramental food of some new religion, since *peyotl*, made from cactus buds, another sacred hallucinogenic agent—but, it seems, not in such early religious use among the Mexicans as mushrooms—has already been sanctified by a 'Christian' church of two hundred thousand members, extending from Central America to Canada.

Not that I should care to enrol myself in any such cult, which would imply ecclesiastic discipline and theological dogma, and force me into friendship with co-religionists not chosen by myself. At school and in the Army, I had my share of that. Modern usage has given the adjective 'anti-social' too wide a meaning. Saints who live alone in their visionary world and acknowledge no friends but the angels or wild animals, may be called anti-social. To broaden the word 'society' by making it include everyone (except, perhaps, criminals), and exact glad-handed mutual love from wholly antipathetic characters, is to make light of the true friendship that *societas* implies in Latin. Many so-called 'anti-social' people are no worse than pardonably careful in choosing their associates. The failure of most churches is due to the weakness of the human bond that supposedly binds their members. Early Christians saluted one another with a holy kiss; for theirs was a society in the true sense, even if from the Roman viewpoint highly anti-social.

The Catholic and main Protestant churches can never, of course, accept visions that either *peyotl* or *psilocybe* excites as anything but diabolical and illusory. They may even put pressure on public-health authorities to outlaw *psilocybe*, arguing perhaps that, although it does not make for addiction among the Mazateks, and seems to have no harmful effect on their minds and bodies, this may be due to its short season and a loss of virtue when dried; whereas the virtue is stable in *psilocybin*, and the results of long-term dosing are unknown—a permanent schizophrenia might occur. Liquor and tobacco interests would no doubt, wholeheartedly support the Churches' plea.

My single experience of *psilocybe*, since it found me in a state of unusual euphoria, was wholly good: an illumination of the mind, a re-education of sight and hearing, and even of touch, as I handled small objects beside me. The perfect sensory control which I could enjoy confirmed, by analogy, my lifelong faith in the poetic trance: a world where words come to life and combine under the poet's supra-conscious guidance, into inevitable and true rhythmic statements. I find one main difference between the two conditions: a mushroom trance is relatively passive; a poetic trance, active—the pen running briskly across the page.

Research should show how far the similarity of most people's visits to Eden or Tlalócan depends on the mushroom's toxic properties, and how far on suggestion. I think it unnecessary, here, to cite Jung's theory of the Collective Unconscious, since a common tradition of Paradise may be attributed to ancient cultural contact even between distant civilizations; especially if these experiences can be shown to correspond with the physical action of a common toxin. A distinct lowering of body-temperature occurs an hour after eating *psilocybe*, which would account for the cool sea-grottoes; and is followed by a considerable heightening of colour and sensitivity, which would account for the jewels. After all, such writhing and creeping things as torment sufferers from *delirium tremens* are clearly not products of the Collective Unconscious, but due to a characteristic tremor of the optic nerve and an irritation of the skin, caused by alcohol.

Tlalócan, in fact, seems to be a subjective vision. As Jesus himself said: 'The Kingdom of Heaven is within you.' He might have added: 'So is the Kingdom of Hell.' The jewelled 'Garden' can be attained by the pure of heart without undergoing so austere a regimen as to become alienated from their friends. The love-feast, for all who attend it in a state of grace and with complete mutual trust—by no means a simple condition—strengthens human friendship and at the same time bestows spiritual enlightenment: which are the twin purposes of most religions. Whether the soul visits a non-subjective Paradise or Hell on quitting its body, let theologians dispute.

The natural poetic trance, however, as I have experienced it on different levels—sometimes light, sometimes so deep that the slightest disturbance causes acute distress—means a good deal more to me than any trance induced by artificial means. I understand Coleridge's depreciation of *Kubla Khan*, which he wrote almost automatically after stupefying his mind with laudanum. It was, as it were, a demon's gift; not earned (like his other poems) by active poetic thought. True, I have had enough operations to know the difference in kind between an opiate dream, where one is the dazed victim, and a mushroom vision that can, I know, be consciously assessed and even controlled. I remember saying to myself at one point while under the influence of *psilocybe*: 'No more Crown jewels: now for something livelier!'—whereupon a group of naked Caryatids appeared; so I hesitate to challenge the claim that Tlalócan, for all its sensory marvels, contains no palace of words presided over by the living Muse, and no small white-washed cell (furnished with only a table, a chair, pen, ink and paper) to which a poet may retire and write poems honouring her—my own peculiar Paradise.

8

Mushrooms and Religion

The profound importance of mushrooms in primitive religion had remained undetected until some twenty years ago, when Mr. R. Gordon Wasson, an American banker, and his Russian-born wife Valentina first called attention to it. The new science of ethnomycology, meaning the attitudes of different races to mushrooms, began with the Wassons' puzzling over the division of Europe into two distinct camps: mycophobes (nations traditionally afraid of mushrooms) and mycophages (nations addicted to eating them). The mycophages of Europe are found in Spain, Southern France, the Balearics, Bavaria, the Balkans and Russia. Russians are the greediest mushroom eaters and recognize over ninety varieties of edible ones.

Until recently we English ate only the white field mushroom *psalliotis campestris*, except in the Midlands where blewets were sold in the markets. But as a boy in North Wales I found even the field mushroom avoided as poisonous.

My mother had spent her childhood in Bavaria where mushrooms grew profusely in my grandfather's pine woods, and when taken there for holidays as a child I soon learned to distinguish seven or eight edible varieties and bring them back to the kitchen for dinner. Home in Wales, I came across some of these same mushrooms growing in the woods and brought them back to eat; but my mother astonished me by shouting: 'Throw those toadstools away at once! Yes, I know that they *look* like the ones we ate last week at Lauzforn, but here they are deadly poison. You had better wash your hands!' Whether she really believed this—her view seemed borrowed from my mycophobic Irish father—or whether she had to take this attitude because the cook would give notice the moment they were brought into the kitchen, I have never decided.

The existence of so many million unreasoning mycophobes throughout Northern Europe and North America —though, to be sure, some of them now dare to accept cooked mushrooms from abroad, neatly bottled—reminds me of another curious taboo in force among the ancient Greeks. They were forbidden to eat any bright red food, such as lobsters, crabs, prawns and wild strawberries (which had no name because regarded as poisonous). The Hebrew word *syeg*, meaning a 'hedge', explains both these taboos. To protect the Biblical ban on, for example, buying or selling on the holy Sabbath, the Jews of Jesus's day had put a protective 'hedge' around the Fourth Commandment by forbidding anyone to carry coins on his person from Friday evening until Saturday evening. And the truth is that mushrooms had once been regarded as holy and reserved for priests, kings and other privileged people; therefore to prevent the unprivileged from eating a sacred mushroom, a general *syeg* was put on mushroom-eating and reinforced by treating all mushrooms as poisonous. However, as already mentioned, an unexplained relaxation of the taboo in England allowed the eating of white field mushrooms, though the most deadly European mushroom of all, the *amanita phalloides*, with which Nero's stepfather the Emperor Claudius had been poisoned, was equally white and has often been mistaken for it. It is therefore reasonable to guess that the sacred mushroom originally protected by these taboos grew in forests, not in fields, and was scarlet; and that the taboo explains the diabolic or disgusting names given even to highly edible other mushrooms.

But why was the scarlet mushroom (which can be

easily identified with the white-spotted one now favoured by red-coated gnomes in suburban gardens and also associated with Father Christmas's reindeer and decorated tree) held sacred? This spectacular mushroom, incorrectly rumoured to be deadly poison, grows by the million all over the British Isles, but only in birch forests. A simple answer is that this was the magical mushroom, on which sat the caterpillar smoking his hookah, that Alice found growing in Wonderland. Lewis Carroll had read about its properties not long before he published the book; they included the same hallucinations about height—'curiouser and curiouser'—from which Alice suffered after nibbling it. This mushroom, named *amanita muscaria*—popularly 'fly agaric'—has now been proved by Gordon Wasson's detailed examination of the Vedic hymns (written in Sanskrit about the time of the Trojan War), to have been the Food of the Gods. It is there named 'Soma'. That it is also 'Ambrosia' and 'Nectar' (both these words mean 'immortal') which were famous as the food and drink of the Greek Olympian gods, I had myself shown some twelve years previously. Two early Greek poets, Sappho and Alcman, had preserved the ancient tradition of Ambrosia as a drink, not a food. This was because the juice of the mushroom—which lost its virtue when cooked—was squeezed out of it between boards, then mixed with milk or curds; and the pulp was thrown away. According to these Vedic hymns, Agni, the god of mystic illumination and holy fire, who was also expressly identified with Soma, had been created when the Father God Indra threw a lightning bolt at the Earth.

Dionysus (Bacchus), the Greek god of mystic illumination, was similarly born when his father the God Zeus (Jove) threw a lightning bolt at the Earth Goddess Semele; the bolt killed Semele but her child was saved and sewn up in his father's thigh, whence he was later granted a second birth. Dionysus is said to have eventually conducted his mother to Heaven where she changed her name to Thyone, meaning 'Queen of the Maenads' (or raging women) and presided over Dionysus's ecstatic October festival, called The Ambrosia. October was the mushroom season. The effect of the *amanita muscaria* taken without other intoxicants is to give the taker the most delightful hallucinations, if he is in a state of grace, but horrible nightmares otherwise. Fortified, however, with beer and the juice of yellow ivy it would send Greek men and women raging mad. A mixture of *amanita muscaria* with whisky has long been used as a celebratory drink by successful salmon-poachers in Scotland. It is called a 'Cathy', in honour of Catherine the Great of Russia who is said to have been partial to it.

The pre-Classical priests of Dionysus, a god now known to have been active in Mycenean times, seem to have claimed the sole rights in the scarlet mushroom, the memory of which they had brought from their original homes in Central Asia and which is not found growing south of the fortieth parallel, except at a great height and always in birch groves. The Vedic priests of Agni seem to have imported their supply from the birch-groves of the high Himalayas. Throughout the world mushrooms were believed to be begotten only by lightning.

That Dionysus was Ambrosia, as his Indian counterpart Agni was Soma, is proved by the legend of his birth from Zeus's thigh. The Vedic hymns make it clear that the priests of Indra and Agni used the two different ways of taking Soma still found among the Palaeo-Siberians called Korjaks, and also in a small Mongol enclave of Afghanistan. The first was a simple drinking of the juice pressed from the mushrooms between boards and mixed with milk or curds. The hallucinogenic *indoles* it contained entered the stomach; but a great many more entered the kidneys and were later discharged with the

97

urine. Clean-minded Classical scholars have until now shut their eyes to the possibility that the Vedic hymn-writer may have meant exactly what he said with 'the great gods piss out together the lovely Soma'. Yet it has been known for at least two centuries that the Korjaks do so after drinking the mushroom juice, and that their friends strain the urine through wool and, after drinking it, enjoy the same ecstasies. And this, of course, explains Dionysus's second birth from the thigh of his father Zeus and his subsequent release to worshippers in a stream of hallucinogenic urine. Yet Dionysus's source of intoxication has always been politely attributed by Greek scholars to wine, and Ambrosia is identified in the *Oxford English Dictionary* with *asclepias* (milk weed); and by various Encyclopedias with almost every sort of plant except mushrooms.

The Norse *berserks* were magicians and sages, and seem to have used the scarlet *amanita muscaria*, as did the Korjaks, for inducing prophecies. They were called Berserks (Bear-shirts) because they worshipped the Bear goddess, which accounts for our Great Bear constellation, and wore bear skins in her honour. Their cult was suppressed in the eleventh century A.D. by Christian converts, not only in Scandinavia but in Iceland, where dwarf-birches in the centre of the island provided the berserks with their *amanita*. The proverb quoted by the Emperor Nero 'mushrooms are the food of the Gods' was true in the sense that they provided the passport to a Paradise from which the mushroom-eater was permitted to return, like a god, after his celestial visions. Yet Nero who, having been excluded from the Eleusinian Mysteries for murdering his mother Agrippina, had not himself visited Paradise, quoted the proverb only in a mocking sense: for his step-father Claudius, after dying from *amanita phalloides* poisoning administered by Agrippina, had afterwards been deified.

I have eaten the Mexican hallucinogenic mushroom *psilocybe Heimsii* in Gordon Wasson's company, with the intention of visiting the Mexican paradise called Tlalócan to which it gives access. The god Tlalóc, who was toad-headed, corresponded exactly with Agni and Dionysus. I also wanted to know whether I had been right in supposing that all religious paradises except the Christian (which is based on a first century Eastern potentate's court), such as the Hebrew, the Sumerian, the Indian, the Mexican, the Polynesian and the Greek (known as the Garden of Hesperides) were not only very much alike but corresponded also with the individual paradises seen by such mystics as the English poet Henry Vaughan, the Silurist. The word *paradise* means 'orchard' in the Semitic languages; an orchard-garden of fruit trees, flowers and running water. Yes, I had guessed right, though there are, I believe, certain dissimilarities: for instance, elephants appear in the Indian paradise and in others the inevitable serpent, familiar to readers of the Paradise chapter in *Genesis*, may appear as it did for me, as an intricately patterned gold chain. A bright snake-like formation is, by the way, a common symptom of a cerebral deoxygenization induced by hallucinogenic drugs; and seeing snakes is a common occurrence among alcoholics, saints who starve themselves, drowning sailors and sufferers from meningitis. My experiences included not only an orchard Paradise where one can see sound, hear colours, and watch trees growing leaf by leaf, but a paradise of jewels like that described in the *Book of Ezekiel* XXVIII, 13–14.

The *psilocybe* mushroom used in the Mexican rites is small, brown in colour, slender-stalked and bitter; but sculptural evidence from Central America suggests that it had supplanted the *amanita muscaria* in ritual use, probably because it was easier to obtain and because the hang-over did not last so long. The same change seems to have occurred in Greece: the discovery of a new hallucinogenic mushroom, a *stropharia*, or a *panaeolus*, which, unlike the *amanita muscaria*, could be ground up and baked in sacrificial cakes for religious use in the Mysteries without losing its powers. When, according to the Greek myth, the Corn Goddess Demeter visited Eleusis, the Attic city where the Mysteries were to be celebrated for another two thousand years, she is said to have ordered Triptolemus, son of the local King, to drive around the civilized world in a chariot drawn by snakes, spreading the arts of agriculture as he went. This myth is clearly deceptive. Corn had been sown and harvested in Palestine for several thousands of years before Demeter's people arrived at Eleusis. What may have happened is that the local priestess sent a message about the newly discovered mushroom to priests and priestesses throughout the civilized world—hence the snakes in Triptolemus's chariot. This, if so, would explain why the nature and source of the original Soma has been forgotten in India for so many centuries. The supply from the birch groves of the High Himalayas seems to have been cut off by enemy action, and *placebos*, such as *asclepias*, substituted for it until eventually its place was taken in Brahman ritual, after the receipt of Triptolemus's message, by a better, more manageable and more accessible sacred mushroom.

In 1957 at my suggestion Mr. Wasson and the famous mycologist Dr. Roger Heim, Director of the Musée de l'Homme at Paris, visited the New Guinea Highlands from whence had come reports of a mushroom cult. They were able to attend a Bird of Paradise courtship ceremony danced by Stone Age men and women under the influence of a sacred mushroom. The specimen that Wasson and Heim were offered proved, however, unhallucinogenic. This may have meant either that the tribal elders deceived their visitors for religious reasons by giving them some ineffective substitute or that the tribe, having emigrated there from a place where a truly hallucinogenic mushroom grew, had been reduced to using this other variety as a *placebo*.

Another variety of the *amanita muscaria* grows south of the fortieth parallel, with the pine as its host-tree, and is equally hallucinogenic. That it was ritually used in Biblical times is suggested by an unwritten Hebrew taboo on mushrooms, broken only by the non-orthodox. (Arabs, by the way, are mycophagous, which perhaps accounts for mushroom eating in those parts of Southern Europe occupied by the Saracens during the early Middle Ages.) I have elsewhere suggested that the golden 'ermrods' laid up in the Ark together with a pot of hallucinogenic manna really represented sacred mushrooms. A concealed reference to their use appears in the *Book of Judges*: the unlikely story of how Samson collected three hundred foxes and sent them into the Philistine's cornfields with torches tied to their tails. The Palestinian fox is not gregarious and the task of capturing three hundred of them, at the rate of one or two a day, and feeding them all until he had collected the full number would have been a senselessly exhausting one. Besides, how could he make sure that the foxes would run into the cornfields and keep the torches alight? The truth seems to be that Samson organized a battalion of raiders—three hundred was the conventional Hebrew battalion strength, as appears in the story of Gideon—and sent them out with torches to burn the Philistines' corn. Indeed, in the 1948 Jewish War of Liberation a raiding battalion was named 'Samson's Foxes'. But why foxes? Because the juice of the *amanita muscaria* mushrooms (which still grow under the pines of Mount Tabor) could be laced with ivy juice or wine to make the raiders completely fearless, and because this variety, when dried, is fox-coloured. So are other mushrooms, such as the popular *chanterelle* which the Russians call *lisichka*, 'little fox'; but to clarify its meaning the Bible specifies 'little foxes with fire in their tails'. In the *Song of Solomon* the Shunemite bride, about to take part in a sacred marriage, urges her lover to fetch her 'the little foxes that spoil the vines, for my vines have tender grapes'. She means that Solomon must fortify his manhood with mushroom-juice laced with wine, the better to enjoy her young beauty.

Why mycophobes called mushrooms 'toad's bread' or 'toadstools' can readily be explained. When the toad is attacked or scared the warts on its back exude *bufonenin*, the poison secreted in the white hallucinogenic warts of the *amanita muscaria*. In ancient Greece the toad was the emblem of Argos, the leading state of the Peloponnese, the emblems of the two other states being also connected with the mushroom: namely fox and serpent. This division into states had been made by a legendary king named Phoroneus, which seems a form of Phryneus, meaning 'Toad-man'. The capital city was Mycenae ('Mushroom City') said to have been built by Phoroneus's successor Perseus ('the destroyer') who, according to Pausanicus, had found a mushroom growing on the site beside a spring of water. The toad was also the emblem of Tlalóc, the Mexican God of Inspiration, and appears surrounded by mushrooms in an Aztec mural painting of Tlalócan, his Paradise.

The Slavs are not mycophobic, probably because their remote ancestors were nomads on the treeless steppes and unacquainted with *amanita muscaria*. Their fermented mare's milk, called kavasse, satisfied their need for occasional intoxication. Like the Arabs in their desert poverty they had learned to eat any growing plant or living animal that was not poisonous. Bavaria is mycophagous, while the rest of Germany is mycophobic, simply because it was once invaded by Slavs.

I should add that reindeer are known to get high on *amanita muscaria* in the birch forests of the far North, a habit of which their owners take advantage.

9

*The Two Births of Dionysus**

Scholars have for centuries disputed the physical identity of Soma, the legendary divine drink celebrated in Vedic poems by the Aryans who invaded India from the North in the second millennium B.C. Some have supposed it to have been alcoholic, suggesting that it was barley-beer, or mead or wine pressed from Afghan grapes; however, the *Rig Veda* allusions to its manufacture do not allow enough time between the pressing and drinking of its juice for fermentation to have taken place. Other scholars have even more impossibly suggested a sort of brandy or whisky—forgetting that the art of distillation had nowhere been invented at that date. A modern Indian view is that Soma was *bhang*, which means 'cannabis' or hemp. Taking cannabis is indeed an ancient enough practice: *cannabeizein*, 'to smoke pot', appears in the ordinary Greek Classical Dictionary. Presumably its fumes were absorbed through the pores of the skin when the cannabis itself was smoked over a low fire—the pot-taker crouching over it clad only in a poncho. This at least seems to have been how the Ashera priestesses of the pre-Reformation Temple at Jerusalem impregnated their skins with the holy incense, which was mixed with other perfumes. But there is no reference in the *Rig Veda* to any smoking. Neither is there any reference to Soma's root, blossoms, leaves or seeds. Yet all scholars have hitherto been searching for a plant, despite the *Rig Veda*'s insistence that it had no root, being divinely born on the high Himalayan mountains.

* *Soma: Divine Mushroom of Immortality*, R. Gordon Wasson: Harcourt Brace & World Inc.

Their favourite choice for Soma has been as *asclepias* or milk-weed, said to be mildly intoxicating, but which grows in the lowlands, not in the high Himalayas. Other guesses are mountain-rue, swallow-wort, moon-plant, moly and silphium.

Gordon Wasson has now made a break-through by identifying Soma without any possibility of scientific or scholarly doubt as a mushroom: the white-spotted scarlet *amanita muscaria* or 'fly agaric' of which the host-tree is the birch, though in low-lying regions below the fortieth parallel it uses pine as its host-tree. Wasson's argument rests on a stark verse in the *Rig Veda* that makes no sense except to botanists, anthropologists and others who have read about the properties of this *amanita*—which Wasson has shown, by the way, to be the hallucinatory one that Alice nibbled in Wonderland— Lewis Carroll having read about it in the *Gardener's Chronicle and Agricultural Gazette* of October 1862.

Before going any further with the argument, I should remind my readers that in 1956 the August *Atlantic Monthly* published a wholly unscientific piece about hallucinogenic mushrooms, written by myself. It was titled *Centaurs' Food* and gave my reasons for supposing that Dionysus, the Greek God of Intoxication, and the only male god who had a part in the Eleusinean and other Mysteries in company with the earth-Goddess Demeter and her daughter Persephone, Goddess of the Underworld, was (like his pre-Columbian Mexican counterpart Tlalóc, with whom he shared almost every divine attribute, including the toad emblem) the God of the Inspiratory Mushroom. I pointed out in that piece that *Ambrosia* ('tabooed food') the food reserved for Gods, gave its name to Dionysus's October festival, celebrated in the mushroom season; and that the initials of the six supposed ingredients of ambrosia (as listed by the grammarian Athenaeus) spelt out (on the cipher principle of Celtic Ogham which seems to have originated in Anatolia) the Greek word for *mushroom*; as also did the initials of the supposed ingredients of nectar, and of *Kukeon*, the drink given to Demeter at Eleusis while mourning for her lost daughter.

As I have mentioned elsewhere the Emperor Nero is recorded to have quoted the ancient Greek proverb that 'mushrooms are the food of the Gods' as a heartless joke about his royal step-father Claudius who had been murdered with *amanita phalloides* and then been deified by the Senate. Yet the proverb referred to a mushroom reserved only for divine consumption, which originally had been *amanita muscaria*. Its sacredness explains, I suggested, the taboo among the early Greeks against the eating of any red foods whatsoever—including the wild strawberry and crustaceans that went red when boiled.

The secret which Demeter sent around the world from Eleusis in charge of her protégé Triptolemus is said to have been the art of sowing and harvesting corn: he drove around revealing the secret from country to country in a chariot drawn by serpents. Something is wrong here. Triptolemus belongs to the late second millennium B.C.; and corn, we now know, had been cultivated at Jericho and elsewhere since around 7000 B.C. So Triptolemus's news would have been no news. He was in fact, I believe, announcing a discovery and a consequent change of ritual. All Paradises—Greek, Sumerian, Mexican, Indian and Polynesian—are much the same the world over, except that the Indian Paradise admits elephants. And each invariably contains a serpent, often appearing in the form of an intricately linked golden chain; supposedly because a bright serpentine apparition is one of the brain's natural reactions to the cutting off of its full oxygen supply, whether by drugs, drowning or stifling. The serpent may be glorious or it

may be frightful. The advanced alcoholic sees snakes.
So do certain sufferers from meningitis. Triptolemus's
secret seems therefore concerned with hallucinogenic
mushrooms, and my guess is that the priesthood at
Eleusis had discovered an alternative hallucinogenic
mushroom easier to handle than the *amanita muscaria*;
one that could be baked in sacrificial cakes, shaped like
pigs or phalloi, without losing its hallucinogenic powers,
and one that did not produce a long hang-over. That the
mediaeval Mexicans had made a similar change is
suggested by very early Central American mushroom
statues which resemble the *amanita muscaria* rather
than the *psilocybe*. Tlalóc's toad emblem confirms this
for me: *bufonenin*, the hallucinatory poison secreted
in the warts of a toad is also found in the white warts of
the *amanita muscaria*.

A few years ago, having learned that certain Portu-
guese witches were using their own variety of mushroom
for magical enchantments, I arranged to have an example
sent to Europe's leading mycologist, my friend Dr. Roger
Heim. It proved, so far as I recall, to have been *panaeolus
papilionaceus*. Wasson has the record. His famous earlier
book, *Mushrooms, Russia and History*, written in col-
laboration with his Russian wife, had made me aware
that *stropharia*, a small mushroom growing on cow
dung, possesses much the same properties, and whispered
news came to me that this was still used for sacred
purposes in India where it grew on the dung of sacred
cows.

Lately I asked a Brahman from South India *why* the
cow was sacred. He answered: 'O, because each part of the
cow is dedicated to one or other of the gods.' 'Yes,' I
said, 'I am aware of that. But do Brahmans on certain
solemn occasions not rely on another product of the
cow?'

Being a Brahman, he remained silent. Which reminded

107

me of a Greek philosophic question: whether an initiate of the Mysteries when questioned about a certain feature in them, by a man to whom it had been revealed in a dream, should answer 'yes' or 'no'? My view is that *amanita muscaria* ceased to be used as 'Soma' in India first because its acquisition from the High Himalayas became difficult, but then because the *stropharia* was a more effective hallucinogen.

Wasson, with whom I have had a continuous correspondence about mushrooms since 1949—it began with a discussion about the Emperor Claudius's death by mushroom poisoning—came to see me in Majorca recently with evidence that my conclusion about the identity of Soma and Ambrosia had been justified. He had shown conclusively that the complicated far-fetched poetic allusions to Soma in the *Rig Veda* could refer to *amanita muscaria* alone: that in fact the earliest hallucinogenic agent at the Divine Mysteries will have been *amanita muscaria*. But my view was that its identity had been so long forgotten because of the Triptoleman change. Wasson consulted me about one *Rig Veda* text that puzzled him, because it did not seem to refer to the *amanita muscaria*, and suggested that it might be a later insertion, referring to some *placebo* for Soma. I reassured him that he was thinking scientifically, not poetically, and that for me this text clinched his argument for *amanita muscaria*; unfortunately I kept no notes of our conversation and he does not mention this incident in his book.

Wasson began his career as a journalist without any university education (which may account for the preservation of his genius), became a Wall Street reporter, was taken over by J. P. Morgan & Co. as their press-agent, and soon elevated to Vice-President when his extraordinary understanding of business became apparent. Similarly with his second profession: he began as an

amateur mycologist and has since become the acknowledged founder of the huge, immensely important new
science: ethnomycology. Whenever I pick up strange
news of mushrooms, as often happens, I send it to him for
filing. It had been a chance piece of information that I
passed on to him in the early Fifties that prompted him
to investigate the mushroom oracles of Mexico. Another
sent him in company with Dr. Heim to examine that
mushroom cult, combined with a bird-of-paradise dance,
in the New Guinea Highlands. Dr. Heim has since
published an account of it.

I make no claim to be a scholar. I get, record and pass
on news and intuitions; but any mention of my work in
academic books is so suspect as to detract from their
sales value and general acceptance. Since, science-wise
(as the Americans say) I do not exist, I having nothing
against Wasson for failing to recall our speculations
about Soma at the time that I wrote my piece about
Ambrosia, Soma's Greek counterpart, in the *Atlantic
Monthly*; or for recording that his identification of Soma
with *amanita muscaria* was forced on him, to his own
great surprise, by a recent reading of Vedic literature!

Now to come back to the peculiar properties of *amanita
muscaria*. Wasson writes:

The fly-agaric is unique among the psychotropic
plants in one of its properties: it is an inebriate in *Two
Forms*.
FIRST FORM. Taken directly, and by 'directly' I mean
by eating the raw mushroom, or by drinking its juice
squeezed out and taken neat, or mixed with water, or
with water and milk or curds, and perhaps barley in
some form, and honey; also mixed with herbs such as
Epilobrium sp.
SECOND FORM: Taken in the urine of the person who
has ingested the fly-agaric in the First Form.

He is here again repeating that, when the mushroom juice is squeezed out and drunk, only some of the indoles which induce hallucinations pass from the stomach into the bloodstream; the rest lodge in the kidneys and there mix with the urine. The urine is filtered, as the *Rig Veda* makes clear, through calf's wool, and then drunk mixed with milk or curds. Not only the Palaeo-Siberians and a small Mongol enclave in Afghanistan—which Wasson visited two or three years ago but where he failed to capture the local confidence—use these two methods of taking Soma. So as I have already remarked do certain Lapps and Finns, who are said to filter and get high on the urine of reindeer that have eaten the *amanita muscaria*.

Since Agni, the Vedic lightning god, son of Indra the Vedic counterpart of Zeus, was also addressed as 'Soma', his identity with Dionysus is now plain. Dionysus had two births: by his father Zeus's lightning bolt which struck the earth—his mother was the Earth goddess Semele—and when his mother died (but was afterwards translated by Dionysus himself to Heaven) he was sewn up in Zeus's thigh and thence born a second time. This is a simple myth to interpret: mushrooms cannot be sown by seed and are everywhere popularly explained as born from a lightning stroke. . . . Also, there are two ways of being inspired by the Soma mushroom: by eating it, and by drinking it (as Wasson explains) after it has been added to the contents of the King or priest's bladder and then released. The identity of Soma and Ambrosia is indeed implicit in the Sanskrit origin of the word 'Ambrosia' namely *a-mrita*, a Sanskrit word for the 'elixir of immortality', which can mean only Soma.

Since Soma has a quieting effect on its takers, the reported wildness of the Dionysian Maenads' behaviour, when eating the same mushroom, must have been caused by its mixture with barley beer, ivy or laurel. The parallels between Zeus and Indra and between Dionysus and Agni are inescapable.

The argument of Wasson's *Soma* is as lucid as unanswerable; the illustrations are wonderful, the quotations numerous and telling. I congratulate him on his feat, and thank him gratefully for helping me finally to reveal the meaning of *Merotraphes* (thigh-nursed), Dionysus's hitherto unexplained nickname. Recently I sent him a short piece explaining Odysseus's use of *moly* in avoiding Circe's mushroom intoxication of his sailors. He has here included a mention of Homeric 'moly', as a possible origin of Soma, but failed to explain—as I did in my note—that Homer (or the eighth century B.C. author of the *Odyssey*) has confused a yellow garlic (which would have the effect of oxygenating Odysseus's blood and thus made him proof against Circe's charm) with wild cyclamen!

Soon after my first experience of hallucination by the Mexican *psilocybe* at Wasson's apartment in New York City in 1960—Jerome Robbins had also been there—I wrote a poem about this but put it in terms of Dionysan, not Mexican, mythology. During the session, the Mexican *curandera*'s litany in praise of the God Tlalóc (disguised as 'Christ') and his divine sister, had been played to us on a tape. It is unlikely that participants in the Soma rite, so long as they were in a state of grace, as I happened to be at the time—for to have a bad conscience makes the participant wish he had never been born —can have had a very different experience from mine.

THE AMBROSIA OF DIONYSUS AND SEMELE

Little slender lad, toad-headed,
For whom ages and leagues are dice to throw with,
Smile back to where entranced I wander
Gorged with your bitter flesh,
Drunk with your Virgin Mother's lullaby.

111

Little slender lad, lightning engendered,
Grand master of magicians:
When pirates stole you at Icaria
Wild ivy gripped their rigging, every oar
Changed to a serpent, panthers held the poop,
A giant vine sprouted from the mast crotch
And overboard they plunged, the whey-faced crew!

Lead us with your song, tall Queen of earth!
Twinned to the god, I follow comradely
Through a first rainbow-limbo, webbed in white,
Through chill Tyrrhenian grottoes, under water,
Where dolphins wallow between marble rocks,
Through sword-bright jungles, tangles of unease,
Through halls of fear ceilinged with incubi,
Through blazing treasure-chambers walled with garnet
Through domes pillared with naked Caryatids—
Then mount at last on wings into pure air,
Peering down with regal eye upon
Five fruited orchards of Elysium,
In perfect knowledge of all knowledges.

10

What Has Gone Wrong?

The human race as such can be traced back some six million years to the primitive man (miscalled *homo oreobates* or 'mountain climber') found fossilized a few years ago in an Italian lignite deposit. Behind him a few more million years return us to another ancestor, a three-eyed lizard, still extant; and behind him we eventually come to single-cell organisms without even male-and-female variation. A question of increasing interest now raised by leading scientists, historians and philosophers, is how the vast changes in terrestrial living conditions caused by an uncontrolled mechanarchy can be halted before the human race is wiped out: the dangers are readily diagnosed, but who will ever be empowered to correct them?

Since these dangers have been introduced mainly by Europeans, and since European pre-history rests squarely on the Greek myths, the best approach to the question 'what has gone wrong?' is perhaps by way of them. The earliest myth of origin preserved by Pliny in his *Natural History*, Homer in the *Iliad* and Apollonius Rhodius in his *Argonautica* makes Eurynome ('Wide Rule') responsible for the Creation of the World from Chaos. In *The Greek Myths* I have retold the story as follows:

In the beginning, Eurynome, the Goddess of All Things, rose naked from Chaos, but found nothing substantial for her feet to rest upon, and therefore divided the sea from the sky, dancing lonely upon its waves. She danced towards the south, and the wind set in motion behind her seemed something new and apart with which to begin a work of creation. Wheeling about, she caught hold of this north wind, rubbed it between her hands, and behold! the great Serpent Ophion! Eurynome danced to warm herself, wildly and more wildly, until Ophion, grown lustful, coiled about those divine limbs and was moved to couple with her. Now, this North Wind, who is also called Boreas, fertilizes; which is why mares often turn their hind-quarters to the wind and breed foals without the aid of a stallion. So Eurynome was likewise got with child.

Next, she assumed the form of a dove, brooding on the waves and, in due process of time, laid the Universal egg. At her bidding Ophion coiled seven times about this egg, until it hatched and split in two. Out tumbled all things that exist, her children: sun, moon, planets, stars, the earth with its mountains and rivers, its trees, herbs and living creatures.

Eurynome and Ophion made their home upon Mount Olympus, where he vexed her by claiming to be the author of the Universe. Forthwith she bruised his head with her heel, kicked out his teeth, and banished him to the dark caves below the earth.

There are not known to have been any gods (as opposed to goddesses) in Europe until the comparatively late invasion of Crete by a flotilla of patriarchal Semites. The event is commemorated in the late myth of how Zeus, in the form of a bull, carried the Goddess Europe to Crete on his back, swimming from Palestine. In fact he did not carry her off: she was a native Cretan and the picture from which the myth was borrowed will have shown her riding him in proof of her domination. Later, a horde of patriarchal nomads from Central Asia overran mainland Greece and took possession of it in the name of their almighty Thunder God Zeus. Greece was an agricultural country and agriculture came under the control of the Goddess Demeter 'Barley Mother'. It was also highly civilized in its crafts, which came under the control of the Goddess Athene. Like Hera, the leading goddess of the Peloponnese, Athene came from Libya and had a totemistic culture: her totem being an owl, as Hera's was a peacock.

After a period in which six matriarchal Greek states under the rule of Hera, and six patriarchal States under the rule of Zeus, agreed to an amphictyony or federation, civil war broke out. The relevant myth presents Zeus as having been bound helplessly to his throne by most of the lesser Greek deities, at the instigation of the Goddess Hera, but presently freed by a monster named Briareus—meaning a group of non-Greek allies from Macedonia and Magnesia. Zeus then revenged himself on his enemies: hanging Hera from a hook on Olympus with an anvil tied to her feet and suitably humiliating all the other deities. This seems to have been the occasion in which Athene—who had not taken part in the war—was forced to disavow her control of handicrafts, such as pottery and weaving, and to claim that she had been reborn from Zeus's head as Goddess of Wisdom.

The original balance of six against six in the Divine Council of gods and goddesses, each with its human representative, was broken in early Classical times with the displacement of Hestia (Vesta) the Hearth-goddess, by Dionysus, god of the Mysteries; women in the Council were now outnumbered by seven to five, and although still allowed participation in their secret Women's Mysteries, took no active part in government. States had been ruled tyrannically by divine inheritance and it was a long time before a changing balance of political parties dependent on votes superseded simple tyranny. Pericles set the pattern. His woman adviser was not a queen, a priestess nor a wife but an untitled mistress.

115

Women's position further worsened when the religion of the Greeks, adopted by their Roman conquerors without radical change, though all but drowned by politics, was superseded by Christianity. The Semitic bull-god El whom Theseus the Athenian deposed in the name of Zeus—when he killed the Minotaur at Cnossus—had become first the God of the Jews, then the God of the Christians and then the God of the whole Graeco-Roman world. Women's inability or unwillingness to control male domination of the arts, sciences, industry, finance and politics, has now allowed the latest and ugliest Palace conspiracy against Zeus to take place. The gods concerned are no longer friendly or noble gods but the scum of Olympus: namely the pseudo-Hermes, god of secret diplomacy, the pseudo-Apollo, god of uncontrolled science and technology, the pseudo-Ares (or Mars) god of the secret police and the Khaki-Mafia, and Plousios the shameless god of Wealth who does nothing to distribute the food-surplus—though he was the son of the Barley Goddess Demeter by Iasion (healer) and begotten in a ploughed field—among the peoples of the world.

The Christian God, whom this junta of divine conspirators is now displacing, and on whom hungry millions call in vain, cannot defend himself by an appeal to women. This is because as Zeus he had earned Hera's undying hatred and because as Jehovah he had concealed his marriage with the Goddess Ashera with whom he originally shared Solomon's Temple at Jerusalem. Men are lost without the magical and protective love of women; and both sexes lose power unless they can take recourse to manual crafts and constant companionship. Machines, while supposed to assist man by time-saving, destroy natural skill and reduce men and women to little better than machines. Former pleasures disappear: few living-houses have gardens, few people know how to

116

cook, few read books, few play games, few take long walks, few think for themselves, few have religious convictions, few love seriously. Very little graphic art except the commercial is now displayed; almost no poetry is written except experimental exercises in the incomprehensible or the obscene; music is played too frequently, loudly and inescapably on the radio and few young people still can sing their parents' traditional songs.

The indiscriminate use of scientific invention without regard for consequences and devoted solely to commercial gain is poisoning earth, sea and atmosphere to a degree which threatens soon to destroy populations by the hundred million. What has gone wrong? The supersession of matriarchy by patriarchy led to the supersession of patriarchy by democracy, of democracy by plutocracy, and of plutocracy by mechanarchy disguised as technology.

Technology is now warring openly against the crafts, and science covertly against poetry. The original meaning of these terms has long been forgotten. Craft in Anglo-Saxon meant 'intelligence', with 'crafty' as its adjective, and applied mainly to manual dexterity in producing useful objects. But in the term 'arts and crafts' craft takes the less important position because art, its Norman-French equivalent, covered the production of a nobler range of objects, just as the Saxon word 'stool' (German *Stuhl*) came to mean a humble chair without a back, whereas 'chair' (Greek *kathedra*) was what the Norman-French gentility used as a sign of their own importance— a stool with back, arms and foot-rest. This social distinction between stool and chair still survives; one is offered a stool of repentance or a dunce's stool, but a Chair of philosophy; and toads sit on toadstools not on toad chairs.

'Technology' is a Greek compound-noun originally meaning 'the topic of craftsmanship', but now meaning 'the application of mechanics to manufacture', and

117

'manufacture', which originally meant a 'making by hand' and usually implied sweated labour, has come to cover the production of goods by almost wholly mechanical means. Thus a home-knitted jersey can no longer be called a manufacture—it is a product of craftsmanship. As for the secret war between science and poetry, one must study their original meanings to make any sense of it. Science, meaning the art of knowing, is the Latin equivalent of the Greek word 'philosophy' meaning 'love of wisdom'. And poetry (it is strange how few scientists are aware of this) comes from the Greek verb *poiein* meaning 'to make or do', which explains 'maker' the early Anglo-Scottish word for 'poet' as in Dunbar's famous *Lament for the Makers*. True poetry makes things happen. Many ignorant young poets must have turned to Aristotle's *Poetics* in the hope of finding a poetic theory discussed there; but of course Plato, Aristotle's master, had banished all poets from his ideal republic and pretended that Greek poetic myth was mere nonsense, not ancient tribal or civic history crystallized in dramatic form. Aristotle's *Poetics* therefore discusses how things are, or should be, made to happen—by any but poetic means. The power of true poetry, as opposed to academic versification, is of a sort that scientists cannot recognize: if only because at its most intense it works in the fifth dimension, independent of time. Several well-known mathematical discoveries such as Rowan Hamilton's Quarternions which came to him suddenly one day as he was walking across Phoenix Park, Dublin, plainly derive from fifth-dimensional thinking: they are not built up from any similar theories but make a leap into the future. Yet scientists would dismiss a similar process in the writing of poems as 'illogical': meaning that the resultant poem does not make a prose sense precise enough to permit exact translation into another language.

118

Some years ago I was invited to give the *Blashfield Address* in New York and took *Baraka* for my subject— *Baraka* is the Moslem sense of blessedness that attaches itself to buildings or objects after years of loving use by noble-hearted people. *Baraka* may seem a foolishly sentimental subject, but few practical people will deny that to break in a new guitar, typewriter or car and as it were humanize it, so that it never lets one down, takes a long time, even if one has used a predecessor of the same make for years previously. And a ship's engineer, especially if he is a Scot, often achieves so friendly a relationship with his engines that they somehow continue to work after apparently irremediable damage.

Science has come to imply a belief in so ordering our civilized life that every citizen will enjoy the same mechanical range of amenities as every other, and as much leisure as he needs: a leisure now usually occupied no longer by entertainment in pubs, cinemas and music-halls but by radio and television in the home. And, closely allied to science and money, technology produces millions of identical and spiritually dead objects which as a rule take far longer to humanize than their expected length of service; whereas unmechanized crafts exercised by individuals or closely knit groups produce objects with elements of life in them.

The worst that one can say about modern science is that it lacks a unified conscience, or at least that it has been forced to accept the power of Mammon. Mammon— or at least the Talmudic 'Mammon of Unrighteousness'— exploits the discoveries of science for the benefit of international financiers, enabling them to amass more and more money and it is hoped, eventually to control all markets and governments everywhere.

In ancient times the use of scientific discovery was closely guarded for social reasons—if not by the scientists themselves, then by their rulers. Thus the steam engine invented in Ptolemaic Egypt for pumping water to the top of the famous lighthouse on the island of Pharos was soon abandoned, apparently because it encouraged laziness in slaves who had previously carried water-skins up the lighthouse stairs. The same with the early invention of the water-mill for grinding corn: it was left unexploited by the Romans for much the same reason as the Pharos pump—all corn had hitherto been ground in hand-querns by slave labour. Still more remarkable was the mediaeval invention of the electric battery by Baghdad Sufis and their abstention from putting it to commercial use for light, heat and power lest it interfere with the traditional arts and crafts. Or take Suetonius's account of how an anonymous inventor came to the Emperor Tiberius, offering to show him a new sort of glass. He dropped a lump of this on the marble floor in front of Tiberius's throne, as if by accident. When it bounced Tiberius asked the man whether he had divulged the secret of its manufacture to anyone, and if so to whom? The man swore that it remained his own, so Tiberius sentenced him to death, remarking that glass of this nature would be found so valuable in the making of jewellery and table ware that it would rapidly depreciate the value of gold and upset the Imperial economy.

Then again, the highly inventive Mexican Aztecs knew about wheels, which they used in children's toys, but forbade their use on the roads lest they should assist a surprise attack on the capital. And although the mediaeval Pyramids, not far from Mexico City, have been cut so exactly that this can have been done only by the use of laser rays, this secret was withheld from the Spanish conquerors and took five centuries to rediscover.

There need have been no war between Science and Poetry, nor between Technology and the Arts, had not the power of money forced too many poor, married scientists and technologists to break what should have been a Hippocratic oath to use their skills only for the benefit of mankind. Money power now also terrorizes leading newspapers throughout the world. Recently I tried to make sense of the Rio Tinto-Zinc/Thorium Inc. decision to stake out claims on the Snowdonia National Park—a district of ancient poetic traditions—for the mining of very low grade copper, though RTZT already owned 900,000,000 tons of high grade copper in Bougainville Island, New Guinea. Yet when I quoted a 21-year-old report in *The Times* (August 27th, 1950) about the high uranium content in the rocks at Dolgellau, which made perfect sense of the RTZT project, no London newspaper, not even *The Times* itself, printed it. A D-notice from security perhaps? The figures were: 2·8 parts per ton of uranium oxide present in a million tons of stone. . . . *The Times* had refused to print on the ground that their lawyers considered the letter libellous. When I asked for details, they were refused me.

More recently the same powerful combine has also gained a legalized footing in the Lake District, open country of more recent poetic associations; but what minerals or rare earths they propose to mine there, I do not know. But here at all events, we find science, manipulated by Mammon, covertly working against poetry, which is how this argument began.

11

Rationality

To be *rational* is not to be *sensible*, which originally meant 'sensitive and aware' as it still does in French and Spanish, but which now means 'unpretentiously thoughtful'. *Rational* does not even mean *reasonable*, which conveys the sense of being open to persuasion by sensible people: it means thinking along prescribed lines without any thought for sensibility in either sense. The difference for instance between real scientists and the routineers of science is that the real ones are *sensible* in the French and Spanish sense; whereas the routineers, being merely rational, have become the destroyers of our civilization.

Though one cannot and should not be rational about love, if only because it is an emotional and therefore unassessable concept, one should be sensible and reasonable whenever its appearance threatens a hitherto settled and agreeable habit of living. Sure tests can indeed be found for recognizing true love from false, but cannot be classed as rational since they apply to irrational situations, and must therefore be neglected by all legal and academic institutions. For example, true love recognizes no alternative. It is not enough for a man to say: 'You are the most beautiful girl I have ever seen.' An Eastern princess once countered this criticism of the past with: 'Ah, but my younger sister is said to be even more beautiful than I'—and then watched her suitor's face carefully. . . . Nor does true love dwell emotionally on the future. 'I would die for your sake' means little; many noble hearts risk their lives for those of ignoble strangers. Even the hope that both lovers will die together is unrealistic: what matters is life, not death.

Nor should love be put to any test: tests imply doubt. Nor should two lovers ever debate which of them is the more important or responsible. Though one of the two may have contributed a three-quarters part in power and wisdom, the whole would be incomplete without the other quarter, which thus becomes three times more valuable in terms of love than any of the other three. True love, in fact, neither plans the future nor presumes on the past, but takes everything as it comes.

All the above may have been sensibly and reasonably written, but not being a poem is unlikely to convince anybody of its truth.

12

The Greek Tradition

Most of the ancient Greeks were farmers in the winter months but became sailors in the summer as soon as the Pleiades had risen. They inherited from the highly civilized Cretans, earlier immigrants of North African and Western Semitic stock, a trade Empire extending on both sides of the Mediterranean from Syria to Spain. Their own ancestry was similarly mixed, including neolithic 'aborigines', perhaps also from the Middle East, and Indo-European pastoralists from beyond the Caucasus. But whereas the Cretans had been content with the use of small offshore islands as trade depots, the Greeks formed a habit of founding colonies dependent on mother cities from which excess of population drove them, myrtle branch in hand. These colonists presently civilized the barbarous hinterland of the shore they had chosen for settlement.

After thirty years in Spain, France, and other parts of the former Greek Empire—especially Majorca, originally colonized by the Rhodians—and occasional stays in Egypt and Palestine, I at last visited Greece proper: recognizing it at once as the true cultural centre of the Mediterranean. The Greeks have always stubbornly remained themselves despite a long humiliating incorporation in the Roman Empire, the suppression by the Byzantine Church of their ancient worship, exploitation by the greedy Venetians, and nearly five hundred years of barbarous Turkish rule. Somehow they kept their ancient language and alphabet, which is more than one can say of any other Mediterranean people—even Israeli Hebrew is a literary revival, not the native tongue of Palestine since Biblical times. Moreover, Greece had taken over the whole Celestial Empire from Babylon and Egypt, renaming its stars: which still continue Greek despite the attempted intrusion of Roman Emperors, Christian saints, and Moslem heroes. The ancient Greek colony of Iope, later Joppa, now Jaffa, a suburb of Tel Aviv, staged the famous myth of Perseus, Andromeda, Cepheus, Cassiopeia, and Draco, whose story spreads over half the night sky. The constellation Hercules similarly recalls not only the Greek colony of Herculaneum on the slopes of Vesuvius, but the two Pillars of Hercules, now renamed Gibraltar and Ceuta. Berenice, whose hair Father Zeus translated to the Heavens, was a Ptolemaic Greek queen of Egypt.

Since Greece is a small country, broken up by deep gulfs, ridged with crisscross mountains, and surrounded by many scores of islands, its national spirit was never that of a horde, as among Northern forest peoples, or of subjects to a divine tyranny as in Mesopotamia or Egypt, but a family spirit of independent loosely federated city-states, each with its own government, coinage, armed forces, festivals, customs, myths. Frequent quarrels occurred between states, but they were always kept in the family and seldom fought to the death. The four-yearly Olympic Games Festival imposed a truce even in war. This state of things continued until Alexander the Great, King of Macedon, a semi-barbarous state in Northern Greece, decided to conquer the Far East, rather than consolidate the Greek colonial Empire, as his father King Philip—a brilliant military tactician—had intended. So he brought the whole of Greece under his autocratic rule and broke the ancient principle of individuality and diversity, in the name of national cohesion.

Each city-state had guarded its myth of origin as a charter of independence, and honoured its founding heroes. These religious myths were yearly represented in dramatic ballets, a long list of which has been preserved by the historian Lucian. And every local custom had its mythological validation: explaining why, for instance, some clans wore only one sandal, why others were forbidden to eat wild asparagus, or trained dolphins for children to ride. Religion was everywhere. No contract could be made, no statue carved, no weapon forged, no vase painted and fired, no building raised, without a religious rite. The twelve Olympian gods and goddesses who officially ruled Greece under Father Zeus had begun as ancestral deities of an early All-Greek federation centred in the Peloponneses. Yet Homer, whose works enjoyed a sort of Biblical sanctity throughout the Greek Empire, had made fun of almost all these Gods except two patrons of the Homeric Guild of travelling minstrels: Apollo and Hermes. Few Greeks could therefore take the Olympian cult seriously, even though it regularized public relations between city-states.

In fact, the Greeks had three interlaced religious systems. These were local worship, the official Olympian cult, and the Mystery cults, such as those of Corinth and Samothrace but especially the Eleusinian cult near Athens. Would-be initiates, who had to be free men with no slave blood in their family histories and without any criminal record, were subjected to long careful screening by priests, then after preliminary induction into the Lesser Mysteries they were taken aside, starved, purged, stripped naked, scared, and, finally, it seems with the help of hallucinogens introduced into the sacred bread and drink, were granted glorious visions of Persephone's Paradise. While still highly suggestive, they learned from the priests of Dionysus, who had control of the rite, a secret doctrine of personal morality which would guide them throughout life and assure them re-entry, at death, into the same paradise.

Homer had never mocked at either Persephone, her mother Demeter, or Dionysus, the three Great Gods of the Mysteries. In fact, we may assume him to have been an initiate. Moreover the Athenian theatre came under Dionysus's own patronage; all the playwrights, musicians, and actors will also have been initiates, and the tragedies seem to present conflicts between public morals, as condoned by the Olympic code, and the secret doctrine taught at the Mysteries.

As Greece grew more commercial, and political power fell into the hands of men either unqualified or unwilling to undergo the ordeals of the Mysteries, religious feeling dulled. By the late fifth century B.C. mercantilism, philosophic theory, and the mechanical sciences had invaded the territory of religion. Buildings became architecturally formalized; statues, no longer archaically carved by craftsmen in a state of divine possession, were turned out in realistic neo-Persian style by matter-of-fact journeymen sculptors; coins became artistically ingenious playthings, not holy objects. Pottery soon also degenerated into trade-ware mass-produced by slave labour for export to barbarians.

A single event marked the final irrevocable decline of ancient Greek tradition. Alexander, after his unpardonably irreligious destruction of Thebes, one of the holiest and most ancient Greek cities, invaded Asia Minor. Having reached Gordium and there been challenged to unpick the complicated Gordian leather knot—a religious task that should be accomplished only by divine inspiration—he sneeringly cut it through with his sword. Then he marched for India, in an attempt to outdo the God Dionysus, who had got no further than Bactria, and on returning to Persia died as a result of trying to out-drink his divine rival.

Whenever imperial dictatorship, philosophic theory, schools of art, and commercialism usurp the religious sense, as has happened again in modern Europe and America, one must turn for spiritual refreshment to the unspoilt countryside, or to museums. Or to ruins—the hand of time and the invasion of wild nature can lend even an ugly Roman-provincial building a certain beauty. I am glad to have seen a few remains of the true Greece, before the new wave of touristic commercialism does for them what, for instance, the Shakespeare cult has done for the town of Stratford-on-Avon; or the cult of sun-tan has done for fishing villages of the once-Greek Costa Brava in Spain.

Recently, by the way, I solved, to my own satisfaction at least, a problem that has long puzzled classical scholars: why all Greek statues of gods and goddesses were originally carved in figwood. The answer was simple: divine statues were always coloured, and figwood was the only sort soft and spongy enough to drink in the dye.

13

Ovid and the Libertines

The word 'libertine', meaning someone who behaves as if free from all moral and religious restraint, is derived from the Latin *libertinus* and *libertina*, meaning male and female slaves who have been released from bondage. Such a gift suggests gratitude for services rendered to their owners in excess of duty; one would therefore expect from libertines a high degree of responsibility and civic virtue. This indeed seems to have been the case with the male libertine. The Emperor Augustus could not rely either on the senatorial class or on the 'equestrians' (mainly businessmen) to undertake the tedious routine of his new Imperial civil service; they would have resorted either to neglect or fraud. Instead, he chose from his own household intelligent *libertini*, mostly Greeks, whom he trusted not to scamp their duty or misappropriate public funds, and whose tasks, though still servile, gave them a comfortable sense of public importance. That the most intelligent *libertinae*, on the other hand, behaved in an altogether different way is so strongly suggested in Ovid's erotic poems that we seem to owe our word 'libertine' to them alone.

What Ovid called *amores* ('amours' to the English) were carefully regulated by Roman upper-class convention. To take advantage of a pretty slave girl in one's own employ was permissible carnality; and it would have been considered disgraceful to show her the least tenderness or special consideration. On the other hand, a secret *amour* with a girl or married woman of one's own class would have been both disgraceful in theory and dangerous in practice; Augustus had, indeed, made it a

129

criminal offence. There remained the *libertinae*. Holding an intermediate position between slave-girls and ladies they provided a corps of skilled and independent courtesans for such well-to-do young men as despised common brothels. 'Libertines', by the way, was the label chosen a few years ago by a vivacious group of Sydney girl-rebels at the King's Cross Red Light Centre, perhaps in a joking justification of their convict descent.

Ovid's *Amores* refer ostensibly only to affairs with women of this sort; *tutior merx libertinarum* ('libertines are a safer buy') as he wrote in his *Satires*. He came of equestrian family, but because the Civil Wars had dangerously thinned the ranks of the old Senatorial order, was chosen among other young men by Augustus himself for elevation to it. After serving briefly as a junior magistrate, he decided to mount no further up the ladder of honours, but to resign his *laticlave* and become a literary man about town. He had two wives wished on him by his family but quickly divorced each in turn, not because they were unfaithful but just because they were in the way. His presumably libertine mistress, Corinna, a tall, elegant, pale-complexioned, passionate red-head, perhaps a Caledonian by race, seems to have been to blame. She was married but Ovid wrote that, fortunately, her husband was unaware of her unfaithfulness to him: his compliance would have made the affair too tame. Nor was she even faithful to Ovid himself who could, he wrote appreciatively, never be interested in women unless like her they took considerable trouble to deceive him. He even professed gratitude to an unknown rival who in his absence had taught Corinna new erotic tricks which she later used for Ovid's own benefit. He seems to have been deeply upset when she became dangerously ill by aborting a child which she said was his; but perhaps because if she had died the husband might have made trouble. He later boasts of never having been involved in a public scandal. Incidentally, Ovid claimed that his poetic advertising of Corinna's erotic capacities had brought her in numerous wealthy customers.

His verses give detailed advice about the exact ambience needed for sexual pleasure; its appetite-whetting preliminaries, the choice of sexual positions to suit partners with different figures, and the advantage to women of a tolerable education in literature and the arts. He must have known well enough that his most faithful readers were neither the *libertinae* (to whom he gave shrewd practical advice about make-up, hair styles, and how to play fast and loose with their protectors), nor even the protectors themselves, but married women of fashion who, bored by husbands who had been forced on them by family arrangement, and treated with as little sexual tenderness as their own slave girls, dared take revenge by carefully schemed adultery. Julius Caesar, Augustus's adoptive father, had been famous for his courage and skill in adulterous intrigue used as a means of uncovering the secrets of his political rivals. He did not even resent the charge of homosexual adventure, and became known as 'every man's wife and every woman's husband'. Yet, as a married man he was extremely careful to protect his own family honour: 'Caesar's wife must be above suspicion.'

The *Amores* are humorous erotic verse essays by a cynical young dandy, who does not take even himself seriously. Somehow surviving mediaeval Church censorship by being written in Latin—a language reserved for scholars and Churchmen—the *Amores* provided our Continental aristocracy with the realistic morality which still rules what remains of them. In France, Ovidian adventures are tacitly excused as venial after a few years of marriage and the birth of children, but no public scandal is allowed to blacken a family's reputation. Romantic love in fact is barred as soon as it threatens to break up a home by decoying the wife away and obliging the husband to divorce her. In Spain the code is slightly different. A husband may keep as many mistresses as he pleases so long as he does not bring them across the home threshold. The wife dares take no lovers: the least whisper of unfaithfulness would prevent her family from ever speaking to her again. The sole exception is when the husband has proved cruel, brutal and an alcoholic, and when the wife is not only very cautious but safely past her menopause.

Romantic love was unknown at Rome until the eighth century, when the Saracens introduced it into Europe after over-running Spain, Southern France, Northern Italy and Southern Switzerland. The word *troubadour* though commonly derived from Southern French *trobar* (to find) is Saracen for 'lute-player'. No attempts to identify romantic love with marriage were made at the time because it implied a harmless poetic flirtation between a lonely lute-player and a woman living in marital subjection to a conventionally brutal husband. In theory she never dared consummate love with him, though stage by stage granting him every possible endearment short of what Ovid realistically considered the only aspect of love that mattered. Several crowned heads were found among the troubadours besides men of low social rank; what mattered most was the poetic intensity of their gratitude for the smallest of their mistress's favours, in fact she was often addressed as 'My Lord'. The word 'mistress' was at that time a term of profound honour. Romantic love, however, soon became discredited by frequent failures on the lover's part to stop short at the required moment; as also happened when mediaeval Irish monks and nuns attempted the same dangerous discipline. Yet the romantic ideal remains enshrined in Arthurian legend and, since marriage in the West is now almost everywhere a

matter of personal choice rather than family arrangement, the twentieth-century tendency has been for
young people to base marriage on romantic ideals.

Marital romance, however, has been so often blighted
by the morbid circumstances of modern life, especially
after the birth of children, that it is now generally discredited. After all, the romantic ideal presents the
woman as the man's mistress in the original sense of one
who rules and directs him; whereas the institution of
marriage is cursed by St. Paul's insistence that the wife
shall be morally and physically in servitude to the
husband. Yet those who identify Church authority with
God and cry out that 'God is dead' find that this amounts
in practice to saying that Love is dead too. As soon as a
marriage bed becomes, in William Blake's words, a
marriage hearse, a natural reaction to Ovidian realism
threatens, especially among the wage-slaves of large,
over-civilized cities. Puritanical delicacy is sapped, and
erotic books and photographs are no longer furtively
peeped at, but now form a main source of income for
reputable publishers; and new refinements of eroticism
are discussed at cocktail parties. Ovid's generalization
post coitum homo tristis ('after coition a man feels sad')
is no longer challenged because simple, affectionate,
trustful love-making has gone out of fashion. Nor has
any convincing solution to the problem of how to recon-
cile marital with romantic love yet been offered.

A new unconventional rendering of the *Amores* has
been made by Joseph Lee, a distinguished Cambridge
classicist, who once won the Vatican prize for a well-
turned Latin poem on the subject of a space flight to the
moon. Deciding that a literal translation into English
verse would be impossible without obscuring the under-
lying sense, Mr. Lee has used brash contemporary
dialect and dispensed with regular metre. This of course
does injustice to Ovid's astonishing skill in handling the

all-purpose hexameter-pentameter couplet. I agree that rides on his rocking-horse soon become tedious and that, as the Victorians said of him, 'his writing abounds with those false thoughts and frigid conceits which we find so frequently in the Italian poets'. The basic difficulty, as with all his contemporaries from Virgil onward, was that he has borrowed his metre from Greek instead of reviving the native Latin stress-scansion used by their predecessor Naevius and by popular Army rhymesters. To write hexameters or pentameters in Latin, which was never meant for quantitative scansion, involved Ovid in countless poetical tricks, evasions and licences; and he is said to have gloried in his virtuosity. A friend once asked, as a favour, permission to remove one single line, the very worst, from Ovid's entire collected poems. Ovid answered: 'Certainly, if I have leave to reserve from excision one single line, my very best.' Each wrote his chosen line on a separate wax tablet: they proved to be identical, namely a pentameter that referred to the Cretan Minotaur who lived in the centre of the maze at Cnossos. Guided by the thread given him by Ariadne, Theseus penetrated the centre of the maze and there found:

Semi-bovem-que virum, semi-virum-que bovem

which might be translated in Oliver Goldsmith style:

> (Led to the centre by the thread
>   Which Ariadne span),
> A half-man bull (he struck down dead)
>   Eke and a half-bull man.

Six of Ovid's lines in Book II XXI of the *Amores* run:

> Femina silvestres Lapithas populumque biformem
> Turpiter adposito vertit in arma mero.

('It was women who caused the woodland Lapiths and the man-horse people (the Centaurs) disgracefully to take up arms when unmixed wine was set before them.')

> Femina Trojanos iterum nova bella movere
> Inpulit in regno, juste Latine, tuo.

('It was women again who made the Trojans wage new war in your land, upright King Latinus!')

> Femina Romanis etiamnunc Urbe recenti
> Inmisit soceros arma-que saeva dedit.

('And it was women who, when Rome had only just been built, caused their fathers-in-law to march vindictively against the Romans.')

Mr. Lee has left out the emphatic 'It was women who' repetition and whittled the passage down to a mere:

> Centaurs and Lapiths brawled
> At Hippodameia's wedding.
>
> Trojans waged war again
> In Latium for Lavinia
>
> Sabines in Rome's infancy
> Fought back to win their women.

Here he could surely have kept far closer to the original without boring his readers: he seems to be somewhat overplaying his part as a hairy-heeled anti-classicist. And by the way, though unattracted by such erotic gamesmanship, I do owe Ovid deep gratitude for the accuracy and abundance of his references to Greek Myths; no Roman poet ever equalled him in that respect.

As a public schoolboy I was taught to pity Ovid, whose indiscretions were so cruelly punished in A.D. 8. Augustus banished him, at the age of fifty-one—after he had happily settled down at last with a third wife—to a hideous one-horse settlement on the Black Sea called Tomi, where even the wine froze. There exchanging his spotless toga for a rough sheep-skin coat and breeches, and the delights of the Capitoline Hill for co-existence with barbarian frontiersmen whose food gave him indigestion and whose language was unintelligible to him, he wrote his *Tristia* (Poems of Sorrow) as an attempt to soften Augustus's heart; but died unpardoned in A.D. 18. Augustus's formal charge against Ovid had been his offences against public morality by the publication of the *Amores*. Though they had appeared some twenty years earlier, Augustus, himself a disgusting debauchee, pretended not to have read them, and banned them, with Ovid's other verses, from the public libraries. It was true, of course, that in the revised edition Ovid had condoned adultery without limiting this privilege to the lower classes, when he declaimed against possessive husbands in general:

Locked up means more desirable. Security
Is a challenge to thieves. Few can love by another man's
  leave.

Your wife's beauty is less of a draw than your passion
  for her—
She's got something special, we think, to hold you.

By being possessive you make her more worthwhile as a
  mistress;
In fact her fear counts far more than her figure.

Storm as you please, forbidden fruit is sweet.
The women who says 'I daren't' is the one for me.

However, you've no right to imprison a free-born girl.
Such sanctions are for foreigners only.

And her warder will say it's thanks to him. Do you
    want a slave
To take credit for her chastity?

To fret about adultery is too provincial
And shows ignorance of Roman manners—

After all, the Martian twins were born out of wedlock
Ilia's children, Romulus and Remus.

Why marry good looks if all you wanted was good
    behaviour?
The two things never mix.

Be sensible and give in to her. Stop being a prig,
Don't press your rights as a husband,

But cultivate the many friends she'll bring you.
You'll reap a rich reward for doing nothing.

Go out when you like to all the gay parties,
Or stay at home and enjoy the presents you never gave
    her.

Nevertheless Ovid's real crime may have been his
amour with too admiring a reader, Augustus's bald but
exquisitely wigged and exhibitionistic granddaughter
Julia. Her father had been the victorious admiral
Vipsanius Agrippa, and her mother, the elder Julia,
was famous for her numerous affairs, though she boasted
that, for the family's sake, she had admitted lovers only
when she was already pregnant. Ovid is said to have
unluckily blundered into the younger Julia's bedroom
while Augustus himself was busy with her. This may
have been mere scandal; at any rate she and Ovid were
banished at the same time. Erotic adventure was, I
suppose, a compensation for the unrelieved boredom of
Roman family life. Still, it is curious how chastely the

Amores read today, even in Mr. Lee's no-nonsense translation, when compared with modern sex classics. And at least he has refrained from fathering any filthy twentieth-century jokes on Ovid, a trick that American translators are now playing on Aristophanes.

14

Birds and Men

Nobody can be sure what early influences affected mankind in its multi-millenary development from whatever primitive living forms have left traces in ancient deposits of sand, clay, chalk or limestone. Yet nobody can deny the influence on mankind, once it became a sort of hominoid, of its amical association with insects and birds. It appears that birds, perhaps the earliest known influence, persuaded men in love to imitate the finesse of cock-birds in their dealings with hens. Man's gallantry during the mating period encouraged him to help with the building of, as it were, a family nest and the feeding of chicks, recognizing these as in part his own. His marital assiduity far outshines that of the male ape— indeed, the latest genetic guess makes man a descendant of what he styles the noble bear, rather than of the ignoble ape. He has even reached a stage of bird-like self-sacrifice. When, for instance, hunters have stolen the eider-duck's eiderdown from her nest, the eider-drake feels compelled to re-line it with his own coarser breast feathers.

Love gifts are apparently another human custom borrowed from birds. The Australian bower-bird prepares as a retreat for his hen a long run ornamented with shining shells, corals, pebbles, coloured feathers and flowers. Similarly, the magpie enlivens his mate's nest with bright objects stolen from dressing-tables and dustbins. Monogamy, as practised by doves, ravens, eagles and other birds, seems to be a further human borrowing, though perhaps a recent one.

Most remarkable of all is bird song, which man has

learnt to imitate and improve to a point where the natural scale, learned from thrushes and blackbirds, is adapted to complex musical composition. The flock discipline of starlings, cranes, and other gregarious birds has also, it seems, been imitated by men for their military manoeuvres. But since man is unlikely to have had any winged ancestors, the thought 'O for the wings of a dove!' is constantly in his stifled heart; and this has finally resulted in the invention of kites, gliders and aeroplanes—never, however, to man's complete satisfaction. The desire to fly with wings, like the Cretan hero Icarus, still recurs in dreams when one flies with arms outspread like birds. Some of us skim only a few feet above the ground, as in the phenomenon of levitation; others soar at the height of tree-tops. This constant dream suggests that the natural flying art will one day be learned by practice. Indeed, cases of levitation have been recorded where a man has flown out of one window and in at another. Some psychologists suggest that flying dreams are really swimming dreams, but I find this far-fetched: one does not swim across one's own garden.

Human self-identification with birds, reflected not only in the procedure of primitive bird-totem clans but in mediaeval heraldry, is followed by social imitation of the ant and the bee. This lesson was first instilled by the Old Testament (*Proverbs* VI, 6 and XXX, 25), although the bee-reference in the first of these texts was struck out at a time when Jehovah's bride, the Mother Goddess in Bee form, had been disowned by His priesthood. The Hebrew prophetess, Deborah ('Bee') who judged Israel under a palm tree sacred to Isis, had saved her people from destruction with the military help of King Barak; but she was only one of a great many Eastern Mediterranean priestesses who ruled the hive on the Goddess's behalf. Her Greek associates, called Melissae (bees), claimed similar prophetic powers. It will be noticed that

140

the revised Scriptures allowed the mention of bees only in pejorative texts (*Deuteronomy* I, 44, *Judges* XIV, 8, *Psalms* CXVIII, 12, *Isaiah* VII, 18). As a result the Queen Bee was regarded by Christians as a King Bee until only five or six centuries ago.

The ant and the bee are several degrees further removed from simple human relationships than birds that migrate in formation, such as starlings, cranes or wild geese. Forcing human beings to conform with the discipline of the hive or ant-hill may be necessary in arid, difficult territory, such as Central Australia, but wherever life is easy to live, seems to be used mainly as a chieftainly convenience for hynotizing slaves to obey their acknowledged superiors.

One habit clearly borrowed by man from birds is dressing in bright colours and showing off during courtship. Peacocks, barn-door cocks and most other male birds are far more brightly-plumaged than hens. Puritanism discouraged this cheerful habit in men at a time when the very act of love had come to be deplored, however necessary it might be for propagation of the race. Modern business men, dedicated to the serious cult of Mammon, still on the whole retain their puritanism of costume, with a special detestation of lace, floppy hats and cavalier-style male tresses. Not that they are less sexually inclined than actors or ballet-dancers. . . . The beard is, however, a difficult problem, and not, of course, connected with bird behaviour. Recently beards have come to express freedom from regimentation, though Napoleon adopted from the Emperor Alexander the prohibition of soldiers' beards—only because in close fighting an enemy might seize his opponent's flowing beard with his left hand and immobilize the head against a blow from his right. This fashion changed for a while after the Crimean War, when soldiers had grown beards because of the difficulties of shaving and because the rifle-and-bayonet kept both hands too busy for any beard-grasping. On their return home the troops were copied by civilians who wished to pass themselves as gallant veterans.

15

The Kaiser's War

When the newspaper placards on August 4th, 1914 read: 'England Declares War On Germany!'—Britain being a word not yet in current use—there was no prouder nation in the world than ours. Though possessing the greatest empire ever known and ruling it, on the whole, humanely, we nevertheless supplemented the national anthem with 'Land of Hope and Glory':

> Wider still and wider
>   Shall thy bounds be set!
> God who made thee mighty
>   Make thee mightier yet!

As successors to the Romans, it suited our governing classes to take over their imperial tradition. The nobility and landed gentry sent their sons to public schools and the major universities for the discipline of Latin, Greek and the birch-rod. The unassuming and ultra-respectable middle classes enjoyed a shorter but more practical education. The profane labouring classes struggled against ignorance and dire poverty, spent a large part of their wages on drink and nursed a stubborn pride in being English. Socialism seemed on the decline: Labour had lost ten seats in the general election of 1910 and now held a mere forty-one. Women could not vote; neither, for that matter, could millions of men with no claim to substantial property—such as the lower ranks in the Army and Navy.

Motor-cars had not yet seriously challenged horse traffic; filthy street crossings were still swept by ragged, barefoot boys for button-booted ladies to negotiate with carefully raised skirts. Electric light was a rare domestic luxury, the telephone rarer; labour-saving devices were limited to carpet sweeper, meat-grinder, knife-cleaning machines and racks worked by a pulley for drying wet clothes over the kitchen range. Aeroplanes in their infancy; jerky, silent, moving pictures enlivened by piano music; no broadcasting; untarred main roads; slums of appalling horror in every big city. A powerful Liberal party; Eire not yet independent; Free Trade; no check on immigration; a minimal income tax; the civil service about one-fiftieth of its present size, working short hours and still using quill pens and red tape; divorces unusual and disgraceful. . . .

We were the envy of the world, especially of our 'German Cousins', who, because of their pre-eminence in music, philosophy and social sciences, believed themselves chosen by God to succeed us. Their temperamental Kaiser, a grandson of our Queen Victoria, had declared that Germany's future lay on the sea, and had undertaken never to rest until her fleet grew as strong as her army —already the most powerful in the world. In 1900, he told German troops sent to defend the Peking foreign legations against Boxer rebels that they must emulate the terrible Huns of old: hence the newspaper use of 'Huns' for Germans. His frequent sabre-rattlings, from the time of the Boer War until the Agadir incident in 1912, his attempt to break the Anglo-French *Entente Cordiale*, and the covetous eye he threw at our colonies, vexed us almost beyond endurance. His excuse for Germany's invasion of Belgium—the murder of an Austrian Archduke in the Balkans—seemed cynically irrelevant. We felt almost relieved when '*Der Tag*', solemnly toasted by German naval officers, dawned at last. Hundreds of thousands of us flocked to volunteer.

Most historians present the war as a sort of chess game

144

between rival Supreme Commands: the united British,
French, Belgian, Russian, Serbian and Montenegrin
commands on the one hand, and the united German,
Austrian, Turkish and Bulgarian on the other. But what
a game! Each group of players in persistent disunity,
everyone new to the game, fresh pieces continually
introduced, and fresh rules extemporized. . . .

None of us had the least presentiment of coming
catastrophe. The Fleet had taken up its battle station at
Scapa Flow; the British Expeditionary Force had landed
in France. Our French and Russian allies were mobilizing
twice as many divisions as the Germans; the Austrian
army seemed a liability rather than an asset to the Kaiser's
forces; Italy had declared herself neutral, and later
joined us. 'War will be over by Christmas.' 'Business as
usual!' Which was like saying: 'The best cure for a
cold is hot rum and a couple of days in bed.'

Memories of the Boer War—only twelve years behind
us—came flooding back. The heroic departure of the
City Imperial Volunteers:

> Duke's son, cook's son, son of a hundred kings:
> Fifty thousand horse and foot going to Table Bay!
> Each of them doing his country's work. . . .

The glorious bonfires of Mafeking Night:

> We're the soldiers of the King, my lads;
> The King, my lads; the King, my lads:
> We shall fight for England's glorious name
> Like the soldiers of the King. . . .

All our generals were cavalrymen, for in this respect
alone the English did not imitate the Romans, who had
treated infantry as their most honourable arm, with
cavalry as mere flank protection supplied by subject
allies. Not until A.D. 378, when Gothic heavy cavalry

broke the legions at Adrianople, had European horsemen counted themselves superior beings. Then arose the Code of Chivalry, borrowed from Islam by our Norman ancestors.

In mediaeval times, King Arthur and his Knights of the Round Table—commemorated in the Order of the Garter—meant more to our chivalrous governing classes than all the saints in the calendar, except their patron, St. George. Every duke had led out his mounted vassals; every peer, his knights; every knight, his rabble of footmen armed with bows, bills and long knives whom he called 'my dear children' or 'infantry'. And blind to change, Generals French, Haig, Plumer, Cavan and the rest still thought of war as a succession of heroic cavalry charges: their territorial gains consolidated by slow-marching infantry.

They made a point of opposing every mechanical innovation that might disturb this dream. They loved horses; they excelled in polo; they hated motor-cars and lorries—nasty-smelling things at which horses shied. Apart from a few traction engines for pulling heavy siege guns, the British Expeditionary Force, or B.E.F. was completely unmechanized until, at the last moment, a couple of Royal Engineer officers were sent round the country to commandeer a score or two of brewery lorries.

No provision had, of course, been made for a supply of magnetos; and the disgraceful story of how the War Office obtained them by secret trading with the Bosch Company of Stuttgart has never yet, I believe, been told! The German army was equipped with 500 lorries, each towing a trailer: Mercedes-Benz, Durkopp and others. Their plan of attack had been prepared down to the last detail.

In late August, the B.E.F., which the Kaiser described as 'that contemptibly small army' (hence the 'Old

Contemptibles'), was forced by the French defeat on its
flank to a head-long retreat from Mons. Small, yes: six
divisions compared with the Germans' eighty-seven.
Yet when in October the Germans—now held at the
Aisne—decided to smother the B.E.F. by a mass attack
at Ypres and seize the Channel ports, they suffered
fantastic casualties from musketry so rapid and accurate
that they mistook it for machine-gun fire.

There were no British reserves, however. By November 14th, our First and Seventh Divisions had been
practically annihilated, and Prussian troops poured
through a gap. They were met by Royal Field Artillery
firing over open sights, and then counter-attacked by a
scratch force: cooks, tailors, transportmen, headquarters
clerks: 30 men from the Second Queen's and 40 from the
First Royal Welch Fusiliers commanded by a second
lieutenant named Orme (just arrived from Sandhurst),
whose death left the battalion wholly officerless. The
Prussians hesitated and dug in. Heavy rain fell, the line
held.

Over half our army had become casualties at Ypres.
The ranks were refilled with special reservists who could
at least form fours and use their rifles. Comfortable
West End clubmen argued that, although the Germans
had overrun all Belgium and a great part of northern
France, and beaten the Russians decisively at Tannen-
berg, they had now shot their bolt. Our French and
Russian allies would soon grind them to powder.

What began as an ordinary old-fashioned campaign,
had taken on, by the spring of 1915, the nightmare
quality of Total War. The period of fluid fighting—
enjoyed by Uhlans, Hussars and Lancers—had ended in
the previous September, and every month of stalemate
now made it more difficult for the Germans to break our
front, which ran from the North Sea to Switzerland.
Formed accidentally by the useless attempts of both

sides to outflank one another, this consisted of a continuous trench protected by barbed-wire entanglements and machine-gun posts; and behind it, support lines, rear lines and tactical reserves.

Both High Commands soon caught the same obsessional madness: a conviction that the enemy line could be breached by intense bombardment with cavalry held in readiness to gallop through, fan out and pave the way for an infantry advance. Presently the German General Staff, still set on capturing the Channel ports, decided to fortify their artillery fire with a surprise weapon banned by the Hague Convention: poison gas.

They tried it on April 22nd at the Ypres salient. The First Canadian Division, its principal victims, did not panic—as their French-Algerian neighbours had done; and the line, though flattened, remained unbroken. This shocking event, and the later German use of flame-throwers, made us all so credulous of German atrocity stories served up by official war correspondents that any compromise peace soon became unthinkable.

Our declared policy was now 'attrition', meaning the daily and nightly bombardment of trenches to weaken enemy morale. That needed an unlimited supply of shells (but David Lloyd George, our new Minister of Munitions, saw to it) and, since the Germans might imitate our strategy, we also needed an unlimited supply of cannon-fodder: namely, conscripts.

We had suffered half a million casualties by the summer of 1915; and at the Battle of the Somme—Sir Douglas Haig's first attempt at a break-through—another half-million. Yet he claimed (untruly) that our losses were inconsiderable compared with the Germans', and the Military Service Act soon swelled his army to a generous million and a half. Haig grudged the divisions sent away to 'side shows'—facing the Austrians in Italy, the Turks in Egypt, the Bulgarians in Greece—

believed that the war could be won only on the Western Front, and wrote in his diary that Almighty God Himself seemed to guide whatever decisions he made.

The British despised Continental armies on the grounds that one volunteer was a match for four conscripts. But in a war of attrition, the volunteer's prowess was seldom put to the test by hand-to-hand fighting. Besides, conscripts soon acquired the appearance of volunteers by wearing the same uniform and sharing the same discomforts.

Each army in turn attempted the knock-out punch: that glorious swing from hip to jaw. Each failed. The most unspeakably horrible, pointless and costly campaign ever fought by British troops was Haig's 1917 offensive. He told the Cabinet that he had 'no intention of entering into a tremendous offensive involving heavy loss', and told his army commanders that 'opportunities for the employment of cavalry in masses are likely to occur'. Although warned by Engineer experts that prolonged shelling of the Ypres area would inevitably destroy the drainage system and return the land to swamp, he subjected the enemy's trenches to a fortnight's bombardment: four and a half million shells. Even this failed to silence the German machine-guns ensconced in concrete 'pillboxes' on higher ground. We made gains of a few hundred yards, but the Engineers' prediction was fulfilled. The Passchendaele battlefield became a quagmire in which not only hundreds of men but even mules were drowned, guns disappeared, and to dig a trench was merely to create a canal. . . . Another 400,000 casualties; yet Haig was not superseded.

He had ridiculed tanks—a British invention—as impracticable toys, and lost their surprise effect on the Somme, in September 1916, by wasting the first small consignment on a purely local gain. It was not until November 20th, 1917, that he permitted a mass attack by 380 tanks across hard ground near Cambrai, without preliminary bombardment. They made an advance of five miles, breaking through to open country; but our cavalry were not alerted and Haig, with no reserves left after Passchendaele, had proudly refused Foch's offer of a French army corps to exploit the breach (which the Germans did not close for several hours).

This was the month of the Bolshevik Revolution, when Russia's armies, our allies, ceased fighting. The Germans would soon be able to transfer two million men from their Eastern front to the West. Meanwhile, they further alienated themselves from the rest of the world by a more serious defiance of international law than poisonous gas. Their submarines were ordered to torpedo merchant vessels on the high seas, including neutrals, without examining their cargoes or allowing the crews time to escape in lifeboats. They even sank hospital-ships, and justified this on the ground that our blockade had been starving children and non-combatants. Thus the United States was eventually brought into the war; but by April, 1917, the Allies were losing nearly one million tons of shipping each month, despite the 3,000 destroyers and other light craft allotted to submarine chasing. Fortunately by autumn our convoy system had reduced these losses to 200,000 tons a month.

England was transformed. Rationing, for the first time in history: unbuttered muffins, wedding cakes without sugar. Golf links commandeered as drill grounds. Country houses turned into hospitals. Servant girls deserting ducal kitchens for the munitions factory. Class distinctions disappearing—as when wounded officers promoted from the ranks fell in love with aristocratic V.A.D. nurses. Zeppelin raids and Boy Scouts blowing the All Clear on bugles. Women enrolled as army cooks, typists, chauffeuses; saluting like men, instead of curtseying. The universities taken over by officer cadet battalions. Expansion of the Royal Flying Corps and the Royal Naval Air Services into the world's largest air force, though suffering immensely high training losses and without parachutes for their crews. 'War babies'; hated war profiteers; despised conscientious objectors. An alarming increase in venereal disease. A sudden boom in poetry after the death of Rupert Brooke. . . .

We were now shouldering the heaviest burden of the war against Germany and her allies. America's new armies being still untrained and short of weapons, the French Army having mutinously refused any more offensives; and the Italians not having recovered from their fearful defeat at Caporetto. Attrition, attrition, attrition! One thousand men killed daily; and a daily £7 million of war debt. Trench life was as obsessive as alcohol. Only in the trenches did we feel free—from generals, staff officers, military police, drill-sergeants, lead-swingers, journalists, civilian bores, patriots or religious fanatics. . . .

But continuous shell fire, and the lesser nuisances of machine guns, trench mortars, rifle grenades, so stimulated our adrenal glands that, after three months, we became mentally off-centre; after six, certifiably insane. We welcomed an occasional ten days' leave; but, if lightly wounded, soon grew bored with hospital and depôt and schemed to get back again, our wounds half-healed. The trenches made us feel larger than life: only there was death a joke, rather than a threat.

The better divisions, which could take up to 90 per cent casualties without breaking, were thrown into every important attack. A soldier who had the honour to serve with one of them could count on no more than three months' trench service before being either wounded or killed; a junior officer, on a mere six weeks. This difference was largely caused by the officer's being condemned, as an honorary horseman, to wear riding breeches and a swordless leather sword-belt, and thus provide a tempting target for German marksmen.

We held two irreconcilable beliefs: that the war would never end; and that we would win it. Eventually it was won, not by us infantrymen so much as by the Navy— which starved the Germans into surrender while they were still occupying Belgium and a great part of France.

At the Peace Conference, God, who made us mighty, made us mightier yet: on paper. The seizure of German Colonies added immense new tracts to our Empire; but we had lost a million dead and as many permanently disabled, besides incurring some £5,000,000,000 worth of war debts. The Americans, who had sent two million men to our rescue and lost 80,000, now led the world. They withdrew from the Peace Conference, left the policing and rehabilitation of Germany to the French and ourselves, and took over our lost foreign markets.

A generation later, the Germans, driven to despair by the wreck of their sacred ambitions, made a second bid for world mastery. Although in Hitler's War our armies were commanded by prudent and capable infantry generals, the subsequent peace reduced us from a second-class power to a third. In the end we were forced to stop thinking like Romans and to jettison all but a few fragments of our Empire.

And how does the official history of the Kaiser's War read? How does it correspond with the personal records and recollections of our soldiers and sailors? I have been reading *The First World War* by Cyril Falls, which is a good deal more than a semi-official document.

Since my great-grand-uncle Leopold von Ranke, the historian, decided that cold facts, after all, deserve a certain reverence, official histories (except under dictatorships) have not been falsified in the heroic Roman fashion set by Livy, but merely slanted. Professor Cyril Falls slants professionally. He served on the General

Staff for most of that war, and afterwards in the Military
History Section of the Committee of Imperial Defence,
then became *Times* military correspondent and Chichele
Professor at Oxford. His *History of the First World
War* explains his view of war as an animated *Kriegespiel*
played between so-called 'great captains'. He quotes no
works written by such well-informed non-professionals
as Alan Moorehead, Leon Wolff, or even T. E. Lawrence;
nor the realistic accounts of the actual fighting given by
Barbusse, Sassoon, Remarque and others. But he does,
on one occasion, concede that Passchendaele was 'grim'.
Generals are the stars, especially *Entente* generals:

> Foch and Haig emerge as the great captains of
> 1918: Foch because he held the Allies together, in
> every sense, by his personality and magnificent fund
> of will-power; Haig because of his refusal to admit
> defeat, his skill on the defensive—shown first at
> Ypres in 1914—and then by the way he accepted the
> main burden of the effort for victory. . . . Both were
> men of unconquerable souls.

Sometimes we are allowed to see that generals could
make an occasional wrong move on the *Kriegespiel*
board, especially enemy generals:

> At a conference before the counter-offensive Luden-
> dorff spoke of the importance of taking the high
> ground about Flesquières from the south-east, and
> with a stroke of a charcoal pencil on the map showed
> how this should be done. Von der Marwitz remarked:
> 'I will take good note of that curve.' As a consequence,
> claims Rupprecht, the Second army made its heaviest
> thrust too far north.

Singularly little mention is made of the Chiefs-
of-Staff, on whose logistics and loyalty every Army

L   153

Commander had, after all, to depend. . . . I am reminded how, shortly after the War, T. E. Lawrence handed me a slim volume of poems, called *Love-in-a-Mist*. I read one, and raised my eyebrows inquiringly. 'Oh, they're no good, of course,' Lawrence said hastily, 'but they *did* cost the lives of twenty or thirty thousand men. He was writing this stuff when he should have been securing the Fourth Army's defences.' Which perhaps explains why Professor Falls insists that General Gough was not personally responsible for the hole made in his line; and did not deserve supersession. The nearest that he gets to uncomfortable revelations is an admission that sea-dogs still grind their teeth to think how easily the German cruisers escaped from the Dogger Bank battle after Beatty's flagship had her signalling equipment shot to pieces and fell behind. But he withholds the inside story of how Beatty's unnamed subordinate came to mess things up. Maybe he was another would-be poet?

The relations between 'Haig, the unconquerable soul' and the 'great national leader' David Lloyd George (who privately called each other 'butcher' and 'cur' and were at daggers drawn) are nowhere touched upon; only a minor 'divergency of opinion' is hinted at. Lack of space cannot be pleaded for this omission, when room is found for such trifles as:

On 6 August Foch was created a Marshal of France. As will appear, he was somewhat busy during the next few weeks and did not receive the baton until the 24th, at his headquarters, the Chateau de Bombon. A vision of swift victory had flashed before his eye one day near the end of July: 'What am I risking, after all?' I asked myself. 'You can prepare for the worst and another year of fighting, but there is no crime in hoping for the best—decisive victory within a few months.'

A full-page photograph of the event shows the Allied Commanders standing stiffly to attention (Haig's riding boots are the most highly polished, and he alone is looking at the camera instead of keeping a respectful 'eyes front'). The cynicism of 'What am I risking, after all?' will not be lost on non-professional readers, particularly survivors of the war in question.

Professor Falls gives the British casualties in the Third Battle of Ypres as 240,000 men, and estimates the German losses at the same figure; adding that Byng's 'finely conceived' subsequent offensive, the Battle of Cambrai, cost him a mere 45,000 men, and the Germans no less. Yet the official figures, published by the War Office in 1922, put British losses from July to December, 1917, as 448,614; and the Germans' as 270,710. Has Falls relied on Haig's optimistic wartime hand-outs? He scorns any notion that the *Entente* leaders should have negotiated for peace in 1916, when invited by President Wilson and the Pope, and urged by Lord Lansdowne; and when the Emperor of Austria and the Kaiser were both ready to treat. The German High Command already knew that they could never win, short of breaking the traditional rules of naval warfare; but that they could bring near-ruin on the *Entente* before actual ruin overtook themselves. Their terms were not preposterous, and capable of being whittled down; hitherto European wars had always ended in close bargaining between statesmen.

Who, then, blocked the road to negotiation? Professor Falls blandly lays the blame for the fatal consequences at the door of 'homo sapiens'! He knows well enough, of course, where the immediate responsibility lay; but his lips are sealed.

16

Fighting Courage

Fear, a reaction to danger common to all animals, though not obvious in plants or trees despite their insistence on survival, has long been punished as a vice in men, boys and hunting dogs and gently ridiculed by men in women. It shows many gradations from uneasy misgiving to blind terror, nor is escape by flight its only recourse. There is also desperate self-defence, often mistaken for simple courage, though in fact no more than a variety of hysteria. A hysterical kitten, threatened by a dog, enhances its fur and spits; a hysterical woman (the word refers properly to mental disturbances supposedly caused by the uterus) screams and distorts her features, threshing her legs and arms. Hysteria is, in fact, a primitive means of frightening an aggressor.

Homer wrote of *chloros phobos*, 'green terror', meaning the corpse-like pallor which precedes a fainting-fit—this being another reaction to danger: a pretence of death, as when the rigidity of horror simulates *rigor mortis*. Fear often causes bowel-movements, probably as an assistance to flight, not as hysteria. In Northern Spain and Southern France peasants in acute danger are said to smell their own corpse-like sweat of terror. Such a smell may well be a primitive reaction to attack by beasts of prey which eat only living creatures: another pretence of death.

The Romans were precise in the words for fear. *Metus* was the simple all-purpose word. *Formido* was innate cowardice. *Terror* was a sudden stroke that scattered crowds in disorderly flight. *Horror* was hysterical fear of the unknown which made the hair bristle. *Pavor*

was cowardice that disturbed the judgement. *Reverentia*
(from *vereor*, 'I fear') was an awe owed to gods or
venerable heroes: the only sort of fear permitted a
young man. Romans did not use the word *panic*, which
originated in Greece where any sudden unaccountable
terror was once attributed to the rustic goat-god Pan.
The Romans identified their own rustic Faunus with
Pan, but admitted to no corresponding Faunal fears.

The death-penalty for cowardice in battle, an established tradition among armed forces throughout the
Western world, is based on the Roman concept of *Virtus*:
which meant fearlessness in defence of one's male honour.
Virtus could also be applied in Latin to the power of
medicinal plants, but Roman women were never
credited with it. The Latin equivalent of our 'womanly
virtue' was *pudicitia muliebris*, 'womanly modesty'.
Napoleon was among the last to use the word *virtuous* in
the Roman sense of *virtuosus*: he wrote that his private
surgeon, who entered every battle so as to give the
wounded immediate treatment, was the most *virtuous*
man he had ever met.

Livy records numerous Roman legends of *virtus*: such
as that of the Consul Regulus captured by the Cartha-
ginians and brought back to Rome by them under
ambassadorial care. The ambassadors hoped that he
would persuade the Senate to sue for a peace, the
signature of which would secure his release. Instead, he
insisted on *virtus* and ordered them to fight on; then
calmly accepted his threatened death by torture—which
was to be rolled down-hill in a tub of nails. Livy also
records the legend of Mettius Curtius: hearing that a
chasm had opened in the Forum and that, according
to an oracle, it would not close until Rome had given her
best to the infernal gods, Mettius mounted his horse and
leaped fully armoured into the chasm, which thereupon
closed over him. 'The best' might have been a Vestal

Virgin, or an honoured matron, or a nobly born child, but the virtuous Mettius knew what the answer must be.

Virtus was a Republican concept. Roman citizens were required to venerate their Praetors and Consuls; but these were officials chosen only for limited terms and no citizen ever appeared before them grovelling in supplication. To fear a Consul, in fact, would have meant either a bad conscience or a personal feud. Compulsory fear reached Rome from the East in Imperial times, when Caligula and Nero, modelling themselves on hereditary Eastern monarchs, reigned by terror with the support of a largely foreign bodyguard. This trend was encouraged by the spread of Christianity. Though Jesus had preached a pacifist creed devoted to a God of Love, his teachings were based on the Hebrew Torah and the early historical books. These attested a God of limitless savagery, who demanded the extinction of his enemies and had to be approached with fear and trembling. When, in the fourth century, the Roman Imperial Army became converted to Christianity from Mithraism and obliged the Emperor Constantine to accept this change, they henceforth fought the good fight with all their might against the heathen, regardless of Jesus's own declaration that such fighting must be left to God's angels.

The bellicose Roman element in Western Christianity has ever since overridden 'Thou shall not kill' and 'God is love'. Any head of state is permitted to declare war on his enemies in the name of God and order his fellow-citizens to kill without mercy. It is assumed that an honest man will never refuse obedience to his superiors in the Church or State even if he has relatives in the enemy ranks, but will nobly face death in battle—his fear of cowardice far exceeding that of death, disablement, or family dishonour. Courage had become a self-perpetuating product of Roman Republican history, and however base and irreligious might be the behaviour of ordinary citizens the Army maintained its *virtus* and discipline, guarded the frontiers, worshipped its Eagle standards and encouraged its veteran centurions to correct unsoldierly recruits with their vine-stock clubs. The Army was divided into legions, its soldiers recruited from distant provinces of the Empire and never stationed in their own. Each legion had a fraternal tradition which supported it in exile and battle so long as its commanders also behaved with *virtus* and pay came through regularly. The backbone of the Army continued to be the infantry until the great Roman defeat at Adrianople by massed Gothic horsemen. Rome's three outstanding generals made their troops unconquerable by personal example of courage—a courage based on an instinctive trust in divine direction, and a readiness to take part in the most dangerous forays or reconnaissances. These were Scipio Africanus, Julius Caesar and Belisarius, all of whom showed their men love and found it reflected back, especially among veterans of their campaigns.

The Biblical text 'Perfect love casteth out fear' is the last word that can be said philosophically, clinically or poetically about fear. But fraternal love cannot be imposed by decree and the British military authorities have often been strangely blind to the source of what used to be called the 'fighting spirit' of the Army, but which half-way through the first World War was typically reclassified as *morale*. This source is a historic tradition of *esprit de corps* in regiments whose colours blazon the names of thirty or forty victories, often beginning in the late seventeenth century. Viscount Cardwell who, as Gladstone's vigorous Secretary for War from 1868 to 1874 abolished commissions by purchase, introduced short service and formed the Army reserve, made the mistake of 'marrying' numerous single-battalion line-regiments for the sake of administrative convenience. He sponsored several glaring misalliances. The marriage between the 43rd and the 52nd Light Infantry Regiments bred particular resentment; the 52nd, though junior to the 43rd and therefore forced to become a mere second battalion of the renamed 'Oxford and Bucks Light Infantry', had an infinitely more distinguished fighting record. Even after sharing a training depot, the two battalions were still on the coldest terms at the outbreak of the first World War forty years later. Further ill-assorted marriages have more recently been forced on even more ancient regiments; but others of no great age and well-known to be of inferior fighting quality have been left alone 'because their depots are centred in successful recruiting areas'. It is no secret which are the real fighting regiments outside the Brigade of Guards: Buffs, Diehards, Gloucesters, Hampshires, for a start. These are the sort that can take up to ninety per cent casualties and still continue in action; others ('no name, no pack-drill' as they say in the Army) are apt to retire after losing a mere ten per cent.

The Turkish army is credited with the highest morale in the West. During the Korean War a company got surrounded and overwhelmed by a horde of Chinese. The surviving officers when instructed to make their men kowtow in acknowledgement of defeat refused and were shot. The non-commissioned officers also refused to give such an order, saying that this was impossible without officers' permission. They too were shot. When the men also refused, one in every ten was shot. In a Turkish as in a British regiment, authority descends in order of rank from colonel to the most junior lance-corporal; and from him to the private soldier with most service. Each is credited with *virtus*. So the oldest soldier, though doubtless he had never heard of the 'drunken private of the Buffs' who faced the same decision in

China, spoke: 'It is no use. You may as well shoot us all.'
This was done.

In English the word 'panic' is more often applied to a
crowd-reaction when fire breaks out or policemen charge,
than to a lonely terror of the unknown. Once a crowd
turns to run, trampling down invalids and children, no
man, however courageous, can arrest the rush. There is
no safety in numbers when fear strikes. *Virtus* is a
personal gift. Yet even *virtus* breaks down when, for
example, an immense explosion occurs without warning.
Dr. William Sargant, in his *Unquiet Mind*, describes
the effect of a German V.I bomb dropped on a first-aid
hospital near London; his medical staff were assembled
in a room close to where it landed. Some of his com-
panions temporarily reverted to what seemed pre-
hominoid escape instincts, burrowing with their fingers
in the cement floor.

Fighting courage in the sense of *esprit de corps* cannot,
it seems, continue to increase beyond the largest number
of fighting men who are personally known to each other
by sight and reputation—say eight or nine hundred,
which is battalion strength—unless years of service are
prolonged, as among the Romans, to twenty or more
years. American attempts to use the division as a unit
for morale do not seem to have been successful in either
World War: its loyalties are too widely dispersed.

17

A Soldier's Honour

Honour in men is their moral mainstay: they can never forgive themselves for showing cowardice in a boxing bout, or a shipwreck, or a battle; or for breaking their sworn oath.

In a Spanish village when the Republic was repudiated by three rebel generals, a newly recruited Civil Guard was told by his captain that the company's allegiance had now been changed by order.

'But Captain, sir, only a week ago I swore an oath of loyalty to the Republic.'

'That may be, but now your orders as a Civil Guard are to swear an oath of loyalty to the new regime.'

'If I break my oath to the Republic what value will my new oath have?'

'Do you refuse to swear?'

'I do, with all apologies, Captain, sir. I apply for my discharge.'

'That cannot be granted. You undertook a five-year service.'

'Of service to the Republic, sir!'

'Be silent, impudence! To the guardroom with you!'

After a night in the guardroom the guardsman was taken out and again ordered to swear the new oath. He refused: 'I never break my oath, and neither did my father or my grandfather, both of whom were guardsmen before me.'

The Colonel was called. He warned the man that unless he took the new oath he would be shot as a traitor.

'As a traitor to whom, Colonel, sir?'

'To your superior officers. We control your destiny here in the Service.'

'But not my honour, sir, pardon me!'

'Tomorrow if you have not changed your perverse mind, you will be shot.'

'I would rather be shot than forswear myself, Colonel, sir.'

He was shot; and it is said that the officer who directed the fusillade could never again face himself in a mirror; nor could any of the soldiers who took part, except those who had never been men of honour for a start.

Oaths sworn to a woman who has never failed in her love for a man, and then broken by him, weigh heavily on a man's sense of honour. So does giving in to the temptation of homosexual self-prostitution.

18

The Absentee Fusilier

Ten years after the first World War ended, *Goodbye to All That* recorded my experiences as a Fusilier officer on the Western Front. Twenty years later, when the second World War had just broken out, I again volunteered for active military service. Since, however, I was now in my early forties, all that the War Office would consent to offer me was a desk job in London. This would have involved bringing my family up from South Devon—and anyhow I had no desk-experience—so I declined. Instead, I volunteered for service in the local Home Guard. This honour was, however, refused me for two curious and contradictory reasons. First that we had two Spanish-republican officer friends staying nearby —escapees from a French concentration camp and therefore suspected as Communist spies. Second, some village joker had carved in big letters on one of my vegetable marrows: 'Heil Hitler!' As the marrow grew, this challenge could be easily read from the road. Nevertheless, I was one day ordered to report to the military authorities at Exeter, being still after all judged young enough for a call-up. They sent me a third-class railway warrant, which I refused on the ground that, as a disabled officer on the Pensioned list, I was entitled to travel first class. . . .

In the end, I was allowed to become an air-raid warden.

One morning as I was busy on a chapter of a new historical novel, *Sergeant Lamb of the Ninth*, I glanced out of the window and shouted excitedly to my wife in the kitchen: 'Look, Beryl, *soldiers!*' She answered with forgivable scorn, 'Soldiers? What do you mean? *Soldiers?*'

And indeed sadly untrained Territorial units of a splendid regiment, the Devons, had often straggled past our house on the Dartmouth road, keeping neither close step nor proper alignment.

I repeated: '*Soldiers!* Look! real ones!'

It was a platoon marching along as correctly as if parading ceremonially on Chelsea Barracks Square. An odd coincidence, at this part of the story, was that our Chief Air-raid Warden, the thirteenth Viscount Falkland, Grenadier Guards, had been the first officer to teach real drill at the Chelsea Barracks. Now, instead of the old-fashioned penal manoeuvring, with criminal faces of 'dumb insolence' roared at by hated sergeant-majors, drill had developed into a splendid sort of all-male ballet. The word 'Order arms!', for instance, was now followed by a gentle but synchronous hand-slap on every rifle butt, and a soundless descent of every rifle.

'Soldiers!' I repeated softly to myself. 'Probably from that new mixed Commando battalion down at Dartmouth!' For I had noticed black-silk Royal Welch Fusilier 'flashes' hanging behind the collars of five soldiers. I went on: 'Once one has seen real soldiers, one is never afterwards mistaken. . . . I bet there are Gloucesters, and Coldstreamers and Koylis and Diehards, and Hampshires too, in that lot.'

Next day I took the boat across to Dartmouth and called at the Commando Mess. There I met Colonel Gilbey of the Welch Regiment (to which I had once been attached) and Major Newman of the Essex Regiment, who later won a V.C. for his Commandos' destruction of the U-boat sheds at St. Nazaire. They welcomed me warmly. Having heard that they were now busy making practice raids on the German-held Channel Islands, I said to Gilbey: 'I suspect, Colonel, that your main problem in raids is how to distract the enemy's attention?'

He nodded pleasantly. I went on: 'Well, as I was coming down here from Galmpton I thought of a device that ought to scare the enemy silly. And so far as I know it has never been tried out.'

'Let's hear about it,' said Newman.

'It would involve sending one of your officers, with a recording machine, to Queen Charlotte's Hospital in West London.'

'Details, please.'

'It's a lying-in hospital. . . . I can't think of anything that troops would be so horribly scared by as the sudden screams and groans of women in labour. . . . Especially Italian troops. . . . Especially on a very dark night.'

Gilbey frowned. 'My dear Graves, I really don't think that would be a very sporting way of fighting our war.'

'No, Colonel, but neither do I think that Hitler and Mussolini have so far been fighting their war over-sportingly.'

Newman broke in: '*I* call it a damn good idea, Graves, but I shouldn't care to use it myself.'

After a short silence we dropped the subject and I congratulated Gilbey on his commandos. 'Their marching order is wonderful—as one expects from volunteers. The real trouble of this war seems to be that we are fielding mostly conscripts.'

*   *   *

Another thirty years passed before I heard the sequel to this story—from an ex-soldier chatting at the table next to mine in our Majorcan village café. He was saying: 'We had our best bit of luck not long before El Alamein. An Eyetie Battalion on our left flank was strongly entrenched and enfilading us. We couldn't advance until they had been moved off, but we had no artillery or air support strong enough to do the job for us. However, one night some bloke from H.Q. showed us a brilliant new idea—I can't say we liked it, but it worked! Just before stand-to, he crept up on them and suddenly set off a record, loud as hell, of a dozen young dames groaning and shrieking together! Sounded like it had been recorded at a lying-in hospital! My God, how those Eyeties ran! The bloke had won us a thousand yards of trench.'

I must say that the news gave me a bit of a turn. . . .

Such was my tactical contribution to the war I never fought.

*   *   *

My strategic contribution to the same war makes another odd story. . . . It starts some time in the early Thirties when Colonel T. E. Lawrence in a depressed mood wrote to me from India, where he was living disguised as Aircraftman Shaw of the R.A.F. He begged me: 'Spare an obol for Belisarius!'

Not understanding the reference, I wrote back inquiring exactly who Belisarius was. He answered that Belisarius was one of the only three really first-class Roman generals in history: Scipio Africanus, Julius Caesar and, five centuries later, this Thracian genius Belisarius. And that Belisarius was the only general in Classical history who had ever successfully invaded Italy from North Africa; but that eventually he was blinded by his ungrateful and jealous master, the Emperor Justinian, and forced to beg for small coins at a street corner in Constantinople. When I also asked Lawrence what made a good general, he summed it up as: 'Never fighting an unnecessary battle and never asking more of his troops than he is ready to give himself —either in reconnaissance or in hand-to-hand fighting.'

Lawrence then suggested my writing a book about Belisarius, none of any value having been published

167

since Lord Mahon's in 1828. In 1938, three years after Lawrence's death, I wrote the book and sent a copy to Winston Churchill. I had known him since 1915— indeed he had been the last man to whom I said goodbye in 1916, at the Admiralty, on leaving for my second long spell in the trenches. He wrote thanking me, adding that he had learned a great deal from my book.

When the second World War was being fought in North Africa, and Rommel had eventually been defeated, General Eisenhower, the Allied Supreme Commander, agreed to Churchill's and Wavell's plan for an allied invasion of Italy. One day I was surprised to read that the expedition had sailed from Africa and landed, like Belisarius's expedition, at Reggio; thence it had crossed the Straits of Messina and, like those sixth-century cataphracts, was steadily advancing up the western coast of Italy.

It may be recalled that Count Belisarius's small forces were fighting a great mass of Germans—the Visigoths. He had, however, soon discovered a crucial rule in German strategy: always to seize the most famous, as opposed to the most tactically important, enemy city— other cities and strong positions could be disregarded. Churchill's strategy was as usual, classical: to follow Belisarius's disregard for all forces on the flank, make straight for Naples, and thence disconcert the Germans by a sudden raid on Rome: two hundred heavily armed men dropped on Rome airport and followed by our main forces.

My friend and bibliographer Fred Higginson of Manhattan, Kansas, was one of the selected raiders and has recently described to me his comrades' surprise and disappointment when the raid was suddenly called off. Apparently, he said, General Badoglio, far preferring the presence of Allied forces in Rome to that of Germans, had been secretly acquainted with the plan but no longer considered it a safe risk to take. Others say that Eisenhower's change of mind was suggested not by Badoglio but by Eisenhower's second-in-command, Air Vice-Marshal Tedder, who nursed a jealous dislike of Montgomery, Wavell and Churchill—all soldiers. Or, more simply, that it was the decision forced on Montgomery by the American General Patton who shared Tedder's dislikes. In effect, the Allied failure to pursue Belisarius's strategy added another three months to the Italian campaign, with immense losses to both the American and British forces. My old comrade Air Commodore Gambier-Parry, who had served as an infantry captain with the Royal Welch in France, had now unluckily been captured by the Germans in Africa, and sent as a prisoner-of-war to Italy. There one day he asked the Mother Superior in charge of Amenities at his officers' prison camp: 'Holy Mother, could you possibly get me an English novel by Robert Graves, called *Count Belisarius*? It is most important.'

'Why important, my son?'

'Because, Mother, it informs us authoritatively how this war is going to end.'

Recently I discussed the question of Tedder's (or Patton's) supposed interference, with Harold Macmillan, the Minister Resident at Allied Headquarters in N.W. Africa from 1942–5. He discounted the story and said that the Germans had struck quicker and harder than Badoglio expected, making the air raid impossibly dangerous. . . . But still I cannot understand why *Belisarius* was voted the most popular novel read by American prisoners in Japanese war camps.

As for the third World War, shall I again volunteer, and again be rejected, and again interfere in its tactics and strategy?

19

The Inner Ear

Ordinary people in the present technological civilization get most of their mental food from their radio or television set, and do not therefore need to cultivate the critical inner ear which depends largely on the eye. Yet, in an age of almost universal literacy, a poem is not a poem until it has been written down and can therefore satisfy the demands of this inner ear which depends on the eye for a full understanding of every line. What is more, true poems are composed in what may be called a 'trance' or a 'brown study', which is the lightest known form of sleep and from which it is most unpleasant to be roused—as Coleridge was roused by the 'person from Porlock' while writing *Kubla Khan*.

It is now generally known that the object of sleep is not so much to relax the sleeper's muscles as to allow him the power of dreaming. And that dreaming means translating, into primitive pictorial or dramatic form, one's recent experiences on the daylight level of logic and reason—thus helping oneself to decide how best to deal with them.

There is a great difference between poems which read well in a public hall and poems which do not. The fact is that the listening outer ear cannot afford to be nearly so selective as the listening inner ear. All day long and part of the night it lies open to a huge variety of messages, seldom addressed particularly to itself, and only a very small part of which it troubles to register consciously, far less evaluate critically. And if ever it does register a message, the evaluation will, as a rule, be on a very low critical level. This phenomenon applies particularly to modern urban civilization: the listener must protect himself against fatigue. Yet a safety mechanism is attached: if one hears a message of immediate importance to oneself—a name, footstep or a word is enough—the recording and evaluating system at once goes into action. And the reading eye practises the same system in reading novels and newspapers: it is called 'skipping'.

I keep no television set in my home and very seldom listen to the radio, or sit in a chattering café where an unnecessary strain is put on my critical inner ear.

20

The Pentagram of Isis

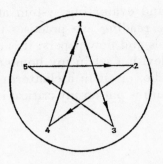

So far as I know, the magical properties of the pentagram, a star-shaped figure which repeats itself endlessly as one traces its five long lines with a pen, across and across, have never been explained in modern times. The pentagram, also known as a pentalpha, was used as a sign of recognition among the Pythagoreans and understood as meaning good health; later the Platonists read it as a sign of good fortune and it is now used as a talisman throughout the world. In Germany it is called a 'Druid's foot'. Its very ubiquity, however, has dulled the mind of scholars and historians to its real meaning, which proves as complex as its form is simple.

The clue will be found by numbering the star points from 1 to 5 in a sunwise direction and then tracing its long lines from point to point until returning to the start. It will be found that the arithmetic difference between these pairs of numbers—between 1 and 3; 3 and 5; 5 and 2; 2 and 4; 4 and 1—is 2, 2, 3, 2, 3. When added together these five arithmetic differences amount to 12, the number of the signs in the Zodiac. When multiplied together, they amount to 72, a holy number constantly recurring in religious myth and legend all the way from

Ireland to the Far East. In Israel, 72 was the number of letters in God's holiest name, and the Sanhedrin had 72 seats including the one left vacant for the coming of Elijah. Its holiness rested not only on 72 as being a multiplication of 8 (the number of solar increase) by 9 (the number of lunar magic) but also—the star-shape not being accidental—as representing the 72-day season during which Venus (the morning and evening star sacred to the Goddess Isis) moved from its maximum eastern elongation to its maximum western elongation.

This use of numbers, like the ceaseless continuity of the pentagram's pattern when its lines are traced from point to point, is relevant only to a single concept: namely the sacred five-seasoned Osirian Year. It never figured in Pharaonic inscriptions—which acknowledged only the Pharaonic Calendar Year of three 120-day seasons—and which was not officially recognized in Egypt until the Ptolemaic period. Pythagoras is said to have studied in Egypt, some three centuries earlier. This Osirian Year had five seasons of seventy-two days each; also a week of ten days (not seven) called an *Asor* and mentioned (*Genesis* XXIX, 27) in the context of Laban and his daughter Rachel.

The Pythagorean use of the pentagram as an emblem of good health was probably suggested by the uninter-rupted movement of the pen from point to point around the calendar year, which lay under the protection of the five deities, Osiris, Horus, Set, Isis and Nephthys. The five seasons represent birth, initiation, consummation, fruitfulness and decline, always followed by rebirth.

Besides these five seasons, the Osirian calendar also contained five extra days, grouped together as a public holiday and sacred to the same five deities. The two goddesses are here represented by two of the numbers in the 2, 2, 3, 2, 3 series, namely the 3 and 3, as the three gods are represented by the 2, 2, and 2—the tradition of male numbers being even, whereas female numbers are odd, is found throughout the ancient world. The five points of the star will have stood for those five extra days. The three-season Pharaonic Calendar contained the same extra days; which were absurdly explained as having been won from Isis by the god Thoth (who corresponded to the Babylonian Nabu, God of Astronomy) at a game of dice—a legend which suggests that the Osirian Calendar was earlier than the Pharaonic and originally, like the planet Venus, ruled by Isis.

It will be noticed that the number 72 also occurs where the five long lines intersect to form five triangles at the star points—the ten angles at the base of these triangles being of 72 degrees each. The name 'pentalpha' (from *pente*, 'five', and *alpha*, the letter *a* which also stood for 'one') probably refers to point 1 from which one's calculations begin. The pentagram's natural representative among growing things is the five-leaved lotus, also sacred to Isis.

In *Gawain and the Green Knight*, a mediaeval English romance borrowed from the Irish, the pentagram is called 'Solomon's Shield' and its five points—which in the story saved Gawain's life—are described as a magic protection against sinful errors caused by the five senses: sight, hearing, smell, taste and touch. Hence the author mentions that its popular name is 'Over-all'. This recalls the Pythagorean description of the pentagram as an emblem of health; indeed, two centuries later its five points are described as sovereign against misfortunes in working, eating, drinking, sleeping and love-making.

The pentagram also answers a seldom-asked question: why are 360 degrees described in a circle, rather than 400 or some other number? Clearly because of the pentagram's convenient approximation of 360, a number multiplying three most sacred others, to the 365 days of the year. The extra five days, regarded as a placatory offering to the five deities, represent one seventy-second of the total sum, plus a few extra hours. And these hours, mythologically represented as the sacred worm which, after three years, grew feathers and became a whole day, a Phoenix chick; and 365 of these days add up after 1460 years to a Phoenix or Sothic Year. At the close of this extra year the now aged Phoenix burns herself to death in a nest of spices at Heliopolis; and from her ashes springs another sacred worm. As I have pointed out somewhere else, it was the Emperor Augustus, by his reform of the Egyptian Calendar, who killed the Phoenix.

21

Solomon's Seal

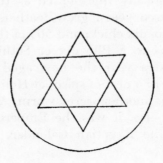

Solomon's Seal (which is the Arabic name for the figure
which Jews call the 'Shield of David', keeping 'Solomon's
Seal' as their name for the pentagram) consists of a
circle surrounding two superimposed equilateral triangles,
and is found on Moslem coins from North Africa. It is
also called, by Jews, the 'Star of David' and has figured
as a distinguishing sign for the victims of pogroms.
The triangle with its point uppermost was regarded as
male; the other, lying reversed, had always been the
accepted hieroglyph for 'woman', because it recalled the
outline of women's pubic hair—men's is kite-shaped
rather than triangular. A superposition of the male on
the female triangle (wherever the sun was regarded as
male and the moon as female) therefore referred to
sexual desire, while the surrounding circle suggested
holy privacy.

The Seal seems to have sanctified a divine marriage in
countries which originally worshipped a Supreme Goddess rather than a Supreme God, but in which (by a
compromise between matriarchal and patriarchal custom)
the executive side of government had been entrusted
first to a lover chosen by the Queen to act as her tem-

porary vizier, and then, after a political revolution, to her husband as a permanent King reigning with the Goddess's consent. At Jerusalem under the early Israelite monarchy, the sacred marriage had been celebrated at the annual vintage Feast of Booths or Tabernacles, between the Hebrew King, representing the Bull-god El (who had been brought down from the North by the Hittites) and the virgin chosen to represent the Canaanite Mother-Goddess Ashera. Hence the *Song of Solomon,* or *Canticles,* which is a sacred love song. After the extinction of the Monarchy and the Jews' return from Babylonian captivity, the King's place at the feast was taken by the High Priest of El, who occupied the sacred marriage couch in the rebuilt sanctuary. Not being of royal blood, however, he remained chaste throughout the feast, though the booths continued to be occupied by countless married pairs whose task was to further the prosperity of the land by cheerful sexual intercourse in honour of El and Ashera.

Yet Solomon's Seal meant far more than an announcement of a public love-feast; when examined closely it proves to be a statement of man's dependence on woman for his well-being, most applicable wherever man is equated with the Sun as power and energy, and woman with the Moon as wisdom and healing.

An ancient Egyptian architectural rule insisted, we are told, that every pyramid should rest on an inverted one of the same proportions. This concealed pyramid plainly represented the power of the Great Goddess by whose divine mercy each Pharaoh reigned, and whose secret authority he acknowledged by a ritual marriage nominally with his own sister but (to avoid incest) with, it seems, a cross-cousin. The shape of the upper pyramid recorded the Pharaoh's domination of the upper world: at his instalment he had shot four arrows with his full strength to the north, south, east and west, and a fifth straight up into the air. But the lower world remained under the Goddess's power, because from the depth of earth rose hidden waters, also sacred serpents and mice, and oracular wisdom. Unless the Pharaoh honoured his goddess wife as royally as she honoured him, the magic of the double pyramid would fail and their joint empire be overtaken by misfortune.

The six points of the Seal represent a multiplication of the female or lunar number, three, by the male or solar number, two; so do the six points of the double pyramid. Moreover, the double pyramid has eight sides, which is two to the power of three, a figure symbolizing increase. Thus Solomon's name is clearly more appropriate for attachment to the Seal than his father David's. David was a fighter and politician, not a mystic like Solomon, whose proverbial wisdom and control of spirits made him famous far outside his territory. Moreover, David had no close connexion with Egypt, whereas Solomon is recorded to have married Pharaoh's daughter and built her a huge palace at Jerusalem; which will have been in fact, a Temple of Isis, or her Canaanite equivalent Ashera, and, as the *Book of Kings* expressively states, very much larger than the Temple he built for his own God El.

Nor was Solomon's Seal merely a dynastic charm. As a two-dimensional sign for the double pyramid it laid down the basic law for all true-love-alliances. This law may be framed in English as 'Man does, Woman is!': which does not deny women their right to activity, but confirms their power to restrain male activity within the bounds that, their intuition warns them, are needed to restrain genocide. In traditional West African monarchies, no King, although in theory absolute, still dares do anything in defiance of his Queen Mother's tearful protests: 'My son, my son, you are killing us.' But without any such love-understanding—and in the civilized world the conspiracy between money, politics and science grows daily more threatening to human survival, nor can any women put an effective brake on male government—we are already on the brink of moral ruin.

22

The Heart Shape

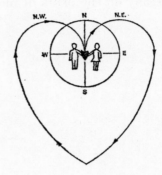

The formal heart shape, of ancient but indeterminate origin, became so familiar throughout the world, because of its inclusion in the pack of cards, that everyone takes it for granted without pausing to wonder how the shape evolved. This heart certainly bears only a remote resemblance to the physical heart, and began, I believe, as a two-dimensional tracing of the Sun's three-dimensional path across the sky, as observed on Midsummer's Day from the Mediterranean or from the temperate parts of Asia. One watches the Sun rise from the north-east, climb steeply by midday to the zenith, then travel round to the north-west until it plunges down below the horizon, reaching its lowest point at midnight, and thence supposedly curving up to the north-east again, where it has been announced by dawn.

This sun path is metaphorical of the light and love which animate a human spirit from infancy to old age; also of the illumined mind's daylong progress in thought until, like the Sun, it dips at last into dream and there refreshes its powers. Whoever really loves is always conscious of the cheerful Sun, even if hidden behind rain clouds or fog, or plunged in the total blackness of night. But the heart-shaped diagram will be incomplete unless the Moon which, unlike the Sun, visits the North has been placed directly above it and thus completed the schematic picture of the limbless human trunk shown from the head to the genitals. Moon and North are associated with wisdom, because to 'sleep upon' a difficult problem implies a decision to solve it: dreams are now explained as a means of solving such problems by a primitive pictorial exercise of thought rather than by ratiocination. And when breakfast is over the wise answer has usually appeared. But the Sun's path should be read as both male and female; the first half shows woman travelling from Wisdom of the North to Glory of the South; the other half shows man making the reverse but complementary journey.

Until only a few centuries ago, as the general Jewish, Christian and Moslem acceptance of the *Genesis* creation story illustrates, Sun and Moon were treated as the Earth's satellites, and it was natural for man and woman to identify themselves contrastively with one or the other of them. Under matriarchy the Sun, as the more powerful and creative satellite, was allotted to woman; which is why in the Irish and German languages, for instance, the Sun has a feminine gender and the Moon a masculine one. Moon-gods and Sun-goddesses were therefore common enough in the Middle East until the patriarchal triumph finally deeded the Sun to man as the dominant sex. Woman was then expected to identify herself with the Moon, if only because of the obvious connexion of her monthly cycle with the moon's; and, indeed, the old English common-law month, a matriarchal survival still on the Statute Book, contains twenty-eight days.

Woman's growing resentment of patriarchy made the

Moon figure as a sorceress, the Sun's jealous opponent. The excuse was her anti-sunwise tendency. Every evening she rose above the horizon a little further to the left, and because of her elliptical course, appeared at irregular intervals of time. This apparent defiance of solar example (the Sun being regarded merely as another, more powerful satellite of the Earth) made the Moon sacred to witches who, at their Sabbaths, danced 'widdershins', meaning anti-sunwise. The Moslems, by the way, also make an anti-sunwise circumambulation of the sacred Ka'aba at Mecca, once the centre of Arabian moon-worship.

An arrow piercing the heart, a powerful symbol, refers to the magical arrow of desire shot by Artemis (or Diana), the archer-goddess, into a man's breast. Its power serves to remind him that, however true he must remain to his honourable daylight calling, he cannot afford to forget Artemis's check on his solar activity, namely the merciful power of woman as Moon, whose function is to provide water for trees, pastures, crops and especially seeds which the Sun's heat has germinated but which are doomed to death without her. The change of sex in the mythological archer, when Artemis was supplanted by Aphrodite's son Eros (or Cupid), resulted from a change in marriage customs. Marriage, no longer prompted by a mutual attraction of bride and bridegroom but arranged by their families for economic or political convenience, encouraged the lover to experiment without restraint in Platonic—meaning homosexual—romance.

William Blake asks in his doggerel rhyme:

> Why was Cupid a Boy
> . And why a Boy was he?
> He should have been a Girl
> For aught that I can see.

For he shoots with his bow
   And the Girl shoots with her Eye,
And they both are merry and glad
   And laugh when we do cry . . .

And answers correctly:

   'Twas the Greeks' love of war
      Turned Love into a Boy
   And Woman into a Statue of Stone
      And away fled every Joy.

Blake is here referring to the famous Theban Band, a regiment of mature soldiers, each paired with a younger homosexual companion, who fought to the death in defence of their country and in honour of their love bond. But as the story of Achilles and Patroclus shows, these relationships were not compatible with heterosexual ones, though rating far above them; and are still characteristic of Greek morality.

The six goddesses of the Olympian Council were reduced to five, and thus outnumbered, by the substitution of Dionysus for Hestia (Vesta); and although their worship was not suppressed they became mere 'statues of stone'. Even Athene who had begun as the early Mediterranean Love and Battle Goddess of North Africa, Greece and the Middle East—Anatha, Anna, Neith and Tanith are her other names—was reborn from the Thunder God Zeus's divine head as a fighting virgin—auxiliary divine male personnel, though admittedly a better warrior than the God Ares (Mars) himself, as Homer's *Iliad* proves.

23

The Sufic Chequer-board

The Sufis' use, for oracular purposes, of the familiar chequer-board with its sixty-four black-and-white squares recalls the sixty-four hexagrams used in the Chinese *I-Ching* 'oracle'. These hexagrams comprise all possible combinations of eight male-female 'trigrams' composed of divided (female) or whole (male) lines. In the black squares a female line will be the undermost of the six; in the white, it will be a male line. Each hexagram is given a special moral meaning when applied interpretatively to a human situation. Yet anyone who wishes to consult the oracle, and thus define his or her own condition by instinctively choosing one of these sixty-four hexagrams, should remember that black and white do not everywhere have the same metaphorical sense. Black in China is treated as a colour and stands for woman (also for the North, where the cautious Sun never shines); and white stands for man and for the South. The *I-Ching* was originally a matriarchal oracle. The divided lines, which represent a woman and the unborn child within her, are therefore considered black. The careful arrangement of this original *I-Ching*, based on a magical square, was broken by Confucius and his friend Duke Chou as a means of asserting the triumph of patriarchy. This is how it had been first conceived:

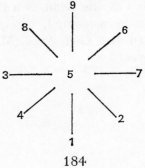

The value of each line crossing the wheel and passing through the hub adds up to 15; 3 and 5 are almost universally considered as creative female numbers. In fact throughout Europe and Asia all odd numbers are female, and all even numbers, male. Among the matrilineal African Negroes, however, the sense is reversed, for the same reason that makes the divided *yin* lines of the *I-Ching* female: a childbearing woman counts as two. This again explains the ambivalent view of twins in Negro Africa. In patrilineal regions twins bring the mother excessive honour, apparently because two raises her original number from even to odd; contrariwise in some matrilinear regions they are regarded as unlucky. And since the Hebrew, Christian and Islamic God, who is of masculine gender, represents absolute unity and is said to emanate a pure white light, all odd numbers are considered male and white by His faithful followers—except where the earlier tradition has survived among mystics.

The Orphic mystics of the Northern Aegean worshipped a black goddess, known as Mother Night, representing order, justice and wisdom, and distinguished her from the white orgiastic love-and-battle goddess. The Orphics' racial origin seems to have been Pelasgian: they came to the Aegean from North Africa about 3000 B.C.

It must also be noted that although there are eight spokes to the wheel, each numbered, and though eight is a male number $(2 \times 2 \times 2)$, the hub is awarded the goddess's creative number 5, which brings the numbers to 9 (3×3).

Among the Sufis, similarly, 'blackness' signifies 'wisdom' because the tri-consonantal Arabic root FHM, with only a minute change in the sound of the H, stands both for 'black' and for 'wise'. This identification is based on the same view of black as is held by the

Chinese, namely that as a pigment it is a concentration of all the existing colours; whereas white is treated as an absence of colour, namely vacuity. The earliest roots of Sufism seem to be in ancient China; and Persia, where the Sufis are first historically noted, had been in the sixth century B.C. the Chinese province of Khorasan. In the Western sense however white is considered as an illuminative rather than as a pigment—a concentration of all the colours of the rainbow—whereas black is plain unilluminated darkness. Thus in English love-poetry beautiful women tend to be fair-haired because 'fair' in English originally meant 'honest'. On the other hand, the Black Virgin statues of Southern Europe were used by Christian-Sufi mystics to represent the Blessed Virgin as St. Sophia, or 'wisdom'. And the famous Black Virgin of Guadalupe was introduced into Mexico by the Spaniards to stimulate the native's faith in a saint of their own dark colour.

The Sufi chequer-board is shown empty—which suggests the limitless possible interpretations of human relationships, not only according as one selects a hexa-gram for self-information, but according whether one interprets black and white in the sense of light and absence of light, or whether in the sense of concentration, or total absence, of pigment.

The chequer-board, moreover, invites the Sufi to a game of draughts or chess which implies a single-minded struggle with his non-self, namely the loveless worldly self induced by the rationality of his daily surroundings. The pieces too are either black or white; so that a choice of colour may denote either the player's sex or his personal religious interpretation of black and white. Since love, it is believed, endows a player with the capacity to see many moves ahead, he cannot fail to win—unless his worldly self has undergone too thorough an academic training.

24

The Nine of Diamonds

Lately I discussed the Scottish superstition that if a folded sheet, back from the laundry, has been accidentally given a diamond pattern at the junction of its creases, one should never spread it on a bed. I explained this superstition (rightly, I still think) as a reference to the nine of diamonds, which is known as the 'Curse of Scotland'; but have since found that I had been wrong to accept the popular tradition which makes the turning up of this card, in a game between a group of Campbells and their unsuspecting Macdonald hosts, the arranged signal for the Glencoe massacre.

The recently published true story given in *The Highland Clans* by Moncrieffe of Moncrieffe (usually styled 'Moncrieff of that Ilk') who is Albany Herald to the Scottish College of Heralds, runs as follows:

On 12 February 1692 the unsuspecting Macdonalds of Glencoe were murdered at dawn in midwinter by the Government troops who had been billeted on them in the most friendly manner for the past fortnight. MacIain, their aged chieftain, was murdered in his bedroom; his widow escaped, stript naked, to die of cold. Their massacre was deliberately engineered by John Dalrymple, Master of Stair, to terrorise all clans who did not agree with his revolutionary politics. He was joint secretary of State for Scotland to William of Orange, who strongly supported the 'plan'. Stair originally wanted to massacre all the Camerons and all the MacDonells of Glengarry as well. Argyll and Breadalbane had necessarily to be

let into the secret of the Government's plan, or part
of it.

The Campbells in general have perhaps received
too large a share of the blame, simply because the
actual troops employed (though very few of the
officers or men were Campbells at all) happened to be
a company of Argyll's* regiment and were commanded by Colin Campbell of Glenlyon. A snowstorm
prevented other troops from coming up in time for the
blame to have fallen more heavily instead on more
senior Government Officers, Colonel Hamilton and
Major Duncanson, who did not belong to Clan
Campbell. It was a Government measure ordered
bureaucratically by progressive Whigs, 'liquidating'
reactionary Jacobites as 'vermin', and a fine example
of 'planning'. The writer is happy to add that it was
Sir Thomas Moncrieffe of that Ilk, as permanent head
of the Treasury, who signed the order for payment of
compensation to the victims of the massacre.

It is known that Captain Colin Campbell did play a
game of cards with two sons of MacIain the Macdonald
chieftain, but that he abruptly broke it off when a
messenger brought the letter from Major Duncanson
with orders from headquarters to begin the massacre.
Colin Campbell secretly spread the word around his
company; but the signal shot was not fired until some
hours later.

The likeliest explanation of the 'Curse of Scotland' is
therefore as follows. The nine of diamonds figures in the
Dalrymple coat-of-arms—in heraldic terms, nine lozenges
on a cross saltire—and it happened to be the last card
turned up before Major Duncanson's letter arrived and
Campbell broke off the game. Campbell read this as an

---

* The Duke of Argyll is still titular head of the Campbell clan.

omen binding him to obedience and putting the full responsibility for the massacre on John Dalrymple, Master of Stair. This self-exculpation, however, will have been not only misheard but misunderstood, so that the 'Fause Campbells' have carried the curse ever since, while the authorities who planned and ordered the massacre, from King William down, escaped all blame.

There was poetic justice at work here. Of all the ancient taboos that bind men of honour throughout the civilized world, the first and strongest is the law of hospitality. Once any man has eaten bread and salt as another's guest, he cannot do him or his household the least injury or dishonour without incurring a curse. Nor can this curse be ended by pleading superior orders. Colin Campbell should have disregarded them at what-ever cost, even at the risk of losing his own life; though indeed the whole chivalry of Scotland, whether Jacobites or King's men, would have stood squarely behind him. The friendly game of cards, the great age of his host, the long wait before the signal gun was fired, the indignity of his hostess's death, all this greatly increased the weight of the curse.

The moral can be clearly read in that superstition of the folded sheet: 'beware of inviting to your guest-room any man who, at the risk of his life, would sacrifice his personal honour in obedience to orders.'

25

Speaking Freely

Interview by Edwin Newman on the
American Air

February 15th 1970

Why even the most spontaneous interviews are unreadable when taken from the recorder, and printed as prose is because they are seldom fresh and unrehearsed discussions between specialists on a single topic and so avoid the stagey intonation that rehearsal induces.

The well-paid interviewer's task is to coax or wring as much off-beat confession as possible from the nervous (and unpaid) interviewee. And if the interviewee is a professional writer he must avoid saying anything which could earn him good money by newspaper publication. The effect even of a bright interview on the sales of his books will be inconsiderable. The popular hero must always be the tactful interviewer; and I confess that I greatly admire Newman's skill.

MR. NEWMAN: Hello, I'm Edwin Newman. Today Robert Graves is 'Speaking Freely'. Mr. Graves, poetry, for you, seems not to be simply a technical mastery of words; but a way of living and thinking. Can you define it?

MR. GRAVES: It's somewhat monastic in a way, bound by all sorts of private rules. So you want to pry into my secrets?

MR. NEWMAN: Yes, very much so, yes.

MR. GRAVES: Well, let's begin from when I left the Army early in 1919, having already published three books of poems, and decided never to be anybody's stooge for the rest of my life. That was rather a boastful decision; but I've never accepted a job since—apart from two professorships. One, five years later, was the professorship of English at Cairo University, Egypt. There I was responsible only to the Vice-Chancellor and I had no predecessors or assistants—in fact I had to buy all the books for the Library. . . . The next job was forty-five years later, when I went to Oxford as Poetry Professor, for private reasons entirely unconnected with the job. There again, I was responsible to nobody except the Vice-Chancellor; and both he and his successor had been undergraduates at the same time as myself, so I had nothing to fear. Apart from that, I have never been anybody's stooge—a very comfortable feeling. What is more, I have never written for any market but my own.

MR. NEWMAN: So you've never written for any market but your own? You really write for yourself? Do you have anybody in mind, then, when you sit down to write? You have written, I find, 125 books, including poetry. Some of them were surely written with a particular market in mind, even if the poetry was not?

MR. GRAVES: A poem is always written for some particular person. And I was asked this same question by Malcolm Muggeridge in a B.B.C. interview.

MR. NEWMAN: I know him.

MR. GRAVES: Good! He asked me: 'Mr. Graves, are the women to whom you write your poems real or imaginary?' And I answered: 'Well, Malcolm, if you want any telephone numbers, you're not going to get them.' That ended that.

MR. NEWMAN: But to elaborate on this point, Mr. Graves, you must have written about what rewards a poet must expect? You set out at the end of the first World War never to take orders from anybody? But you do, in effect, take orders from your personal Muse, surely? The character whom you call the White Goddess?

MR. GRAVES: That's rather a difficult question. I spent ten years writing a book called *The White Goddess*, and the other day, reading the *Sunday Times*, I found myself listed amongst the thousand 'Makers of the Twentieth Century'—in the G–H section, along with

191

Goebbels, Goering and Hitler. I wondered what I'd done, and found that I had written *The White Goddess*. It was not my only book, but had just got around a bit more than the rest. And 'The White Goddess' is a historic character: the goddess of love and battle, the goddess of life and death, who ruled Europe long before any male gods appeared here. She was a hard task-mistress and kept her male subjects in very good order; until eventually they broke allegiance after the arrival of our Indo-European ancestors from Central Asia, who were cattle people. Cattle people have gods, not goddesses, for the simple reason that the bull rules a herd, and that the cows count on him for protection. Any challenger for the headship has to meet the horns of the king bull; so also with cattle kings and their challengers. Those cattle people did no planting, but simply drifted from one pasture to the other. The whole fertility mystique in Europe and other parts of the world where nomadic patriarchal herdsmen are not found, is dependent on agriculture. The woman's job is to plant, sow and harvest. She alone has the right touch, is at one with nature and knows exactly what to do. So, when these two opposed cultures mix, there's great confusion at first.

The White Goddess had to keep firm control of men; otherwise they would soon have got out of hand. And she did so for a long time. Few people realize that this same Goddess, under the name of Ashera, was in charge of Jerusalem until long after the earlier books of the Bible had been written; and that she had a temple on the Temple hill about five times the size of Jehovah's. And that she took all political decisions herself until she found at last that she could no longer trust men, and decided: 'Very well, let them see how they can manage by themselves.' And so she retreated. She is still always there privately for those who need her, in the person of the Virgin Mary or of the woman whom one adores;

but politically she has stepped aside and let men make a mess of things.

I was asked to give the annual address at the London School of Economics recently, and was rather puzzled why. They asked me to name my subject. So I told them: 'Mammon'. They wrote back complaining that they did not know what Mammon was. I thought it a little odd: must I explain simply that Mammon was the Hebrew word for money and that the Talmud was quite clear on the subject? There are two sorts of Mammon: the Mammon of righteousness and the Mammon of unrighteousness. In the Gospels, only the Mammon of unrighteousness is mentioned. And the Mammon of righteousness was exemplified when Abraham bought the cave of Machpelah from Ephron the Hittite to be a burial place for all Israelite patriarchs descended from him—that was a righteous use of money. Then came the unrighteous use of money, when Joseph's brothers sold him to the Midianites in the desert. Money, in fact, was neither good nor bad in itself at the start but must be put to good use. What eventually happened was that money ceased to be either good or bad, and became just bad—a self-sufficient and conscienceless god.

MR. NEWMAN: Do you think this is because we have gods rather than goddesses?

MR. GRAVES: Women always say: 'I'm such a fool about money.' Meaning: 'I don't want to hear anything about it because it's a bad thing, however convenient at times. As soon as you work for money and nothing but money, you might as well be dead.'

MR. NEWMAN: Well let me, if I may . . .

MR. GRAVES: That's a poetic view, and unarguable.

MR. NEWMAN: Well, all right; let me push on with it! You've taught—you said you've only twice been a professor, but you have nevertheless lectured at a number of American universities.

MR. GRAVES: I get around, yes, because I'm interested in what's happening in America.

MR. NEWMAN: After one visit you spoke of 'those talented, beautiful, well-groomed, studious girls and their dreadful, ignorant loutish escorts with nothing to talk about except the ballgame.'

MR. GRAVES: That was at . . .

MR. NEWMAN: Now, if in this unfortunate money-directed society the men are mostly louts, how do the women escape being so?

MR. GRAVES: Escape being *louts*? 'Lout' is a male term. That was some years ago. I don't know what's been happening since. And to judge from some of the characters who come here, what you call 'loutishness' seems to have caught on pretty well.

MR. NEWMAN: What I'm asking is: in the society which we now live in, which is god- rather than goddess-dominated, do women come out of it better than men do?

MR. GRAVES: (*pause*) I'd like to have notice for that question. It's too big a one.

MR. NEWMAN: You once said: 'If I were a girl, I'd despair. The supply of good women far exceeds that of the men who might deserve them.' Do you . . .

MR. GRAVES: Oh, yes I do. . . . The fact is that for one reason or another homosexuality among men has gone so far that it's very difficult now for a woman to find a man who isn't in some way tainted with it. I suppose that it's partly due to heredity, partly to environment, but largely because men now drink too much milk.

MR. NEWMAN: Really?

MR. GRAVES: It's a fairly widespread medical view.

MR. NEWMAN: Well, that would make homosexuality rampant in the United States . . .

MR. GRAVES: The percentage is, I read, about twenty times what it should be. Normally, it's about 1·5 per cent

194

of the population. Homosexuality was recognized by the American Indians: they had *bardashes* who had been allowed to decide at the age of thirteen or fourteen that they wanted to become women. So they were allowed to dress and behave as such. Fair enough! What happens now is that men pretend to be men but are not. And wives soon find that their husbands are really more interested in the other thing . . . which is enough to break up almost any home.

MR. NEWMAN: Mr. Graves, is your supposition, or belief, that plentiful milk drinking causes homosexuality, based on intuition or on what we call scientific observation?

MR. GRAVES: On objective reasoning. Unfortunately a lot of men gain the confidence of unsuspecting girls by being partly women themselves. They learn all the dirty tricks that used to be played by women on nasty men, and use them against women.

MR. NEWMAN: Do you despair of American society? For example, you wrote quite recently about—this is a quote—'the marked decline in native American genius since the turn of the century', you were then blaming it on the educational system which, you said, was too logical. In your view—and you go to the United States quite often—are we in serious danger? I ask this question very seriously.

MR. GRAVES: I think the young people are all right, in so far as they haven't drunk too much milk or allowed themselves to be drugged into imbecility—as too many of the weaklings have—but there's a good base of sense among the best of the young. Oddly enough, they know far more about mathematics than my generation, and also more than the intermediate generation. I like them, I must say.

MR. NEWMAN: Of course, the United States is a country where what we call urbanization has gone very far—though possibly in England it's gone just as far. You think urbanization is a very, very unfortunate thing, do you not? You don't like living in a city yourself and you think city life has a very bad effect on most people and in particular on poets? Is that right?

MR. GRAVES: The two things don't go too well together.

MR. NEWMAN: Then let's talk about urbanization, and about the values that city life creates. You say, for example, that most modern American poems are dull because most American poets live in cities.

MR. GRAVES: I have said nothing of the sort. I say that the whole craftsmanship of poetry has gone down the drain, throughout the country, in the same way as craftsmanship in painting has gone down the drain. In painting academies you're allowed to paint how and what you like, and claim that it's glorious and wonderful. And if you can persuade a gallery to buy your pictures or sculptures, very well, that proves it. As for poems, the actual quality of writing has enormously declined since the time of, say, Robert Frost and E. E. Cummings, who were both very, very careful writers. There are one or two real poets still around—I won't name them, so as neither to encourage nor discourage them—who are working honestly and well. But as Robert Frost once said: 'It's fun playing tennis without a net, but it's not so good a game.'

MR. NEWMAN: And that is what . . .

MR. GRAVES: If you're writing a poem and you want to have any effect on your readers . . . though you should not really be thinking of your readers, but only of yourself as your own reader—you've got to put them under the hypnotic trance in which you yourself write poems. And you impose this trance by certain hidden technical aids in the use of words and language; but to find this out takes years and years. If I write a poem and feel dissatisfied with it—which I almost always am—I re-write it anything from five to thirty-five times.

Twelve is a good average. I finish the draft at night; in the morning I wake up and it looks quite different. So I have been doing the repair work in my sleep, and I now know more or less what's wrong. This may happen three or four nights running, the poem getting each time more and more like what it was originally going to be.

MR. NEWMAN: This is something which you impose on yourself: the trance in which poetry is written?

MR. GRAVES: One doesn't impose it; one suddenly finds it . . . have you ever suffered from migraine? Well, I suffer from frequent migraines. In fact, I've written a poem saying that love is a universal migraine. Now, where was I? I've interrupted myself.

MR. NEWMAN: You were talking about the trance in which poems are written and the technical methods by which the trance may be induced or imposed.

MR. GRAVES: The poem attacks you in the same way as a migraine does. You are looking at a page and all at once you can't read clearly and you realize you've got a migraine. Gradually the whole bright semi-circle of light expands, and you can see nothing. Which is how a poem starts. It forces itself upon you, and then you must go on fighting until it's gone.

MR. NEWMAN: Do you sit down every day in the hope that inspiration will come, or with the intention of inducing it?

MR. GRAVES: No, a poem is completely unforeseeable. Very often one is deceived and makes a mess of things; it doesn't very often happen, but usually the poem comes out all right, if you persevere. But it must have that clear internal order in which every single word corresponds with every single other—and, remember, words must not be treated as counters, which usually happens, but as living things. Now, here I have this thirteen-volume *Oxford English Dictionary*, and also that *Slang Dictionary* and that *English Dialect Dictionary* in six volumes and *Noah Webster* and Latin, Greek, Welsh, Irish, French, Spanish, Majorcan and German dictionaries. I'm always thinking about the history of words. Every word carries a long history of usage with it, and combines creatively with thousands of others all along its line. A poem is a most fantastic experience.

MR. NEWMAN: Mr. Graves, if that is the case, does one improve as a poet as one grows older? Since there is always more to call on?

MR. GRAVES: Most poets have finished by the age of twenty-three. It's very rare indeed for anyone to go on until the age of forty-six, as Shakespeare did. It's still rarer to find a case like Hardy, who stopped writing poems for several decades then picked it up again in his sixties and went on to the eighties. As a rule, poetry is part of one's adolescent love affairs only.

MR. NEWMAN: Are you saying there, sir, that people stop writing, or that they simply don't write as well after youth has gone?

MR. GRAVES: They don't write poems.

MR. NEWMAN: They don't write poems at all?

MR. GRAVES: No, they don't write poems, though they often write verse. They cease to be poetically alive.

MR. NEWMAN: In your own case . . .

MR. GRAVES: Forty-six is the dangerous year.

MR. NEWMAN: Forty-six?

MR. GRAVES: Forty-six is the year in which most people have nervous breakdowns; be very careful. . . . I won't ask your age!

MR. NEWMAN: I don't have to worry about that any more but . . .

MR. GRAVES: Anyhow, forty-six—that was once the age in which everybody was due to die and still is in the jungles of Africa. And it was so in England in Elizabethan days.

And Nicholas Lord Vaux, quoted by Shakespeare, wrote: 'I loathe that I did love in youth that I thought sweet' at the age of forty-six. He said: 'For age with stealing steps hath clawed me with her crutch, And lusty life away she leaps as there had not been such . . . The noble shroud . . . the winding sheet. . . .' He was ready for the grave. And so was Shakespeare when he retired at that same age. Now, forty-six (be very careful) is the age when businessmen have nervous breakdowns. They go off to a hospital and at the end of a year or two they feel recovered. They want to come back but as a rule they've lost their jobs. It's very cruel.

MR. NEWMAN: In your own case, Mr. Graves—which I think it is impossible to avoid asking about—forty-six was nearly thirty years ago for you, and you are certainly still writing poetry. And twenty-three was more than half a century ago.

MR. GRAVES: I was never afraid of death—having already officially died of wounds in France on my twenty-first birthday—and I was never afraid of losing my job—I hadn't a job to lose.

MR. NEWMAN: Does moneyed success spoil a poet?

MR. GRAVES: People say there's no money in poetry: but on the other hand there's no poetry in money. And I used to be careful once never to make more money on my poems than would keep me in cigarettes. And then— well, my numerous children and grandchildren had to go to college, and I eventually found out, to my surprise, that the detritus, the residue, the cast-off stuff, namely the work-drafts, were worth far more than the published poems. So I was able to send those children to college and live quite well myself by selling what I might easily have thrown away but had kept. Why I kept my drafts is easily explained: it was because when one gets to the end of a poem, one looks back to make sure that nothing important has dropped out on the way. I put the drafts aside, and let them pile up; and finally sent them up to the attic.

MR. NEWMAN: Has it helped you, Mr. Graves, that you've had two families? I know you have said that it is a very good thing for there to be considerable distance in years between parent and child.

MR. GRAVES: Well, you've just seen my son, Tomás—he's sixteen and I'm now in my seventy-fifth year. I became a great-grandfather two years ago—but I don't take it too seriously. Old age is a pure illusion. (*pause*) Centuries are like men. We start off with tremendous ringing of church bells when the New Century comes in—everything's going to be wonderful! And then we have sympathetic growing pains and by the Forties or Fifties we settle down into the century. After that, things turn nasty. And by the time the century reaches threescore and ten we can expect 'labour and heaviness' as the Psalmist said. And everyone starts worrying what's going to happen in the year 2000 with the population explosion and a general break-down. All that one can say is that nowadays there are glasses manufactured to improve your sight, which was denied King David when he wrote about the labour and heaviness due at the age of seventy. And now you also can get dentures. The Father of the United States, General Washington, invented and made them himself . . .

MR. NEWMAN: Of wood, I believe.

MR. GRAVES: Yes, and the only trouble was that he couldn't control the spring, so that his mouth was always in danger of flying open. That's why he got the reputation for such noble taciturnity. But anyhow, what the century wants now is sight: in order to investigate its personal problems and find out exactly who is befouling the state. We all know quite well who he is really, but we don't say so. We also need teeth to implement our laws; we're now in the Seventies, and I hope that these Seventies bring us teeth and eyes, not only in America but in Britain, which I left forty years ago.

MR. NEWMAN: Mr. Graves, to what extent can a poet engage in non-poetic activities without impairing his talent?

MR. GRAVES: It's a question of whether he gets cotched.

MR. NEWMAN: Cotched? oh, 'caught'!

MR. GRAVES: Caught, that's right, yes. This world is getting bound more and more closely in the same system. One takes a job and finds that one must be loyal to one's organization, even if it means being disloyal to other allied organizations and to other countries and even, quite often, to one's relations. I should hate having to decide, if I found myself part of some organization that was acting in some way or other against my own personal morality, whether I should stay or go. Often one can't afford to go because of a sick wife, or a large family or this, that and the other. So one has to stay; and that's an ugly thing to face. Innumerable people have to live by what I call 'The Lie': in fact the whole misery of modern life is largely due to people realizing that they're no longer true to the standards in which they were brought up. Admittedly some of the standards in which children get brought up nowadays are pretty permissive.

MR. NEWMAN: What about political activity for a poet, Mr. Graves?

MR. GRAVES: Nothing doing! You may occasionally have to call on a Prime Minister and read him the riot act. Do you have riot acts in America?

MR. NEWMAN: Oh yes.

MR. GRAVES: You do? Well, a poet may be forced to go about things in a pretty strong way. You remember that Shelley talked about poets being mankind's unacknowledged legislators? So people have asked me: 'Well, are you a poet?' And I answer: 'Nobody can claim to be a poet; that will be decided only when he is dead.' They say 'You don't deny being one—have you done anything recently in the way of legislation?' I say, 'As a matter of fact, early this year there was a notice in *The Times* that the most important judicial decision made in the past year was in the case of Parsley v. Sweet.' Did you ever hear of Parsley v. Sweet?

MR. NEWMAN: No, sir.

MR. GRAVES: Well, a girl called Stephanie Sweet . . .

MR. NEWMAN: May I just interrupt for a minute to say that Parsley v. Sweet is in the United States Parsley versus Sweet?

MR. GRAVES: Parsley versus Sweet? Very well. Sergeant Parsley was a very pleasant bucolic Oxfordshire policeman who brought a case against Stephanie Sweet, a graduate of Oxford University, who happened to be a college chum of my daughter, but was had up on a charge of managing disorderly premises. In other words, she had rented a country house which, having only about a month of rent left to run and a broken-down car, she lent it to some friends' friends and didn't care what happened there, so long as they paid her the cash. They turned out to be a group of pot-smokers. So Sergeant Parsley made things very unpleasant for Stephanie, poor girl, who found herself in a magistrate's court on a charge of managing a disorderly house: namely a place where drugs were taken. She asked my advice and I told her: 'Do *not* plead guilty!' Her lawyers wanted her to plead guilty, but she took my advice. And I said, 'Okay, I'll help you through, whatever this costs.' The magistrate's court found her guilty, although acknowledging that she didn't know that her sub-tenants were pot-smokers. She appealed to the Divisional Court. The Divisional Court pronounced her managing of such premises to be an absolute crime, and denied that she could lawfully make any appeal against conviction. When I heard that Stephanie had become an absolute

criminal, I said, 'Okay, we'll go to the House of Lords—
the supreme Tribunal. It doesn't matter what this costs,
you must go through with it.' So we got hold of Rosie
Heilbron, Q.C., the smartest woman lawyer in England.
Rosie went to the Lord Chief Justice and said: 'Look
here, my lord, what's all this about? It is against Common
Law to be found guilty of a crime which you do not
know is a crime.'

Eventually he considered the case, and five Law Lords
to none voted for a change in the law. So now nobody
can be convicted of managing a premises unless it can
be proved he knew what was happening there and had
profited from the knowledge.

MR. NEWMAN: So you have put through some acknowledged legislation then?

MR. GRAVES: It was never acknowledged to me. . . .
Sergeant Parsley was very, very much annoyed that his
name was given such prominence and that I had called
him a very bucolic character. But it had to be done,
first of all, by publicizing it in the *Sunday Times*.

MR. NEWMAN: So you think it's permissible, then, for
poets to engage in certain non-poetic activities, when the
issue is strong enough?

MR. GRAVES: It was a question of justice, which is closely
connected with poetry. Stephanie Sweet was a school-
teacher, and she had been sent a letter from the Minister
of Education warning her that she must not teach again
until she'd been to a head-shrinker. As stupid as that!

MR. NEWMAN: Mr. Graves, let's take a larger subject.
Some American poets, many American poets, many
American artists of various kinds, are deeply involved
in politics in the United States—very largely, I think,
because of the war in Vietnam. Is that likely to affect
them—affect their work—do you think?

MR. GRAVES: If you protest against the war in Vietnam,
you've got to realize what you're protesting against.

Who had broken what moral law? It's not enough to say 'I don't like war.' Nobody likes modern war. The important question is: who is doing what? About a ton of American bombs is supposed to have been dropped every twenty yards throughout Vietnam. Has it? A lot of cruel and conscienceless things have been done, but how do we know that all those many bombs have been dropped? Who is making the money out of their manufacture? Did all those bombs really exist? There are a lot of questions to ask. When the American forces cleared out of France, they found that the enormous pile-up of bombs that they had been asked to remove simply weren't there—and the discrepancy was never explained.

MR. NEWMAN: But these bombs, if they had been dropped in Vietnam, had presumably exploded—so they would not be still recoverable?

MR. GRAVES: No. But on the other hand, if all that are claimed had been dropped and all had exploded, there wouldn't be any Vietnam left. It's difficult to know where you are, you see. One knows—I've heard all about the officers' rest camps in Singapore. I had an English girl-friend who took a good look at one. . . . Well, as people say, 'Isn't it just too bad?' And people who protest against war naturally want to know who makes the money and who is doing what. Strictly speaking, it isn't even a war. War hasn't yet been declared and never will be, because that would bind the U.S.A. to keep to the letter of the Quadripartite Pact which forbids killing of civilians, poisoning of soil and water, and other uncivilized tricks. It's officially called a 'police action'.

MR. NEWMAN: What do you think is the responsibility of a poet? Is he, perhaps, as you earlier quoted from Shelley, an 'unacknowledged legislator'? In your own case, you were in uniform for a long time in World War I, and had a very terrible war.

MR. GRAVES: It was a nice clean war.

MR. NEWMAN: Clean?

MR. GRAVES: Well, until almost half-way through. Then it became anybody's war because it started getting dirty.

MR. NEWMAN: The question I'm leading up to is: since the conduct of nations and the activity of nations can bring about wars, to what extent . . .

MR. GRAVES: Police actions, please! There's not been a war declared for the last twenty years.

MR. NEWMAN: My question is: to what extent is anybody —poet or not—entitled to opt out of public activity and out of the activity by which government policies are made? Whether you call them wars or police actions or whatever. How do you justify a private withdrawal from political life?

MR. GRAVES: The English tradition of poetic morality, such as it is, comes through the Norman French, from the Welsh, and eventually from the Irish. And curiously enough, the Irish poetic morality was very much dependent on the East, because Ireland got its priests not from Rome but from home, and they were responsible only to the Patriarch of Antioch. But never mind that! Any evasion of sworn international pacts—such as that of making war, and breaking all its rules, and saying this is merely a police action . . . it simply would be unpatriotic to support a government that cannot keep its oath.

MR. NEWMAN: Have we got off the track? Or I . . .

MR. GRAVES: Perhaps we're both off the track. So this morality—which I claim to be English, though it can be traced back through Ireland to the east—implies that nobody, whatever happens, must be allowed to act against his own conscience. And that a poet must denounce falsity wherever denunciation is called for. But it remains a purely personal act. It's no good waving

flags, fifty abreast and shouting: 'We don't like war.'
That's not practical. One must show who's been cheating,
who's been lying, who's been making the money in what
unjust business. And the poet must pin-point it. . . . If
everybody acted poetically there wouldn't be any more
nonsense. Sometimes a poet can take action.

MR. NEWMAN: Mr. Graves, you said earlier in this
interview that you no longer fear death, because you
have already once officially died.

MR. GRAVES: Yes, and so have a lot of other people. But
would you like to know how crazy I am? (*Mr. Newman
laughs*) Well, I have come to agree with my advanced
mathematic friends who now agree that time is only a
convenience, having no absolute sense. So when one
does any real thinking—take, for instance, Rowan
Hamilton, the young Irish mathematician who invented
Quaternions back in 1842. . . . He was strolling across
Phoenix Park, Dublin when suddenly this important
formula came to his head. He happened to have a pen-
knife with him, and cut the formula in stone on the
bridge across the Liffey, now called Quaternion Bridge.
Quaternions are among the chief mathematic props in
nuclear physics. How can one dart nearly a hundred
years ahead of time?

The simple answer is, time doesn't exist. People
often plead, 'It was not my fault'—blaming their
parents for giving them a difficult childhood, and so on.
I take sole responsibility for having been born. My
parents never chose me, because they knew nothing
about me and had no idea which of their own genes
I'd choose, what I'd look like, what sort of life I'd live. . . .
Then who *did* know? It's no good saying 'God' because
God is surely a mere question mark? So I say: 'I arranged
it all myself!' Now, to make yourself responsible for
your entire life, and all your stupidities, successes, ill
luck, joys and sufferings, puts you in a very strong

position, because you can blame nobody else. But the question arises: when were these decisions taken? Obviously you didn't exist *before* your time, although you can mentally go back in time and forward in time, which is quite a common experience among clairvoyants. Then precisely when did I make myself? . . . At the moment of my death.

MR. NEWMAN: At the moment of your death?

MR. GRAVES: Why not? That's the only time when one's life is complete. And of course, when you're dying, your whole past life is said to come flooding in with precise memories. Very well! That gives you a neat package all tied up. Yet it has not yet happened, and from the point of view of people living in other solar systems it won't happen until millions of years hence.

MR. NEWMAN: You had an experience happily denied to the vast majority of people. You were . . .

MR. GRAVES: Why 'happily'? Scores of my friends got killed.

MR. NEWMAN: I say 'happily' because—because you were badly wounded.

MR. GRAVES: Listen, I'm seventy-five, and I'll still run you a hundred yards. No? you won't?

MR. NEWMAN: Your own attitude to time and to what comes after, happens to be expressed in a poem that I was going to ask you to read. It expresses your view of whether a poet should think about what honours are coming his way.

MR. GRAVES: Well, fame can be very useful if you're crossing a frontier and you want to take something questionable through the Customs. Otherwise, it can be an awful bore.

MR. NEWMAN: Well, you helped us get some equipment into Spain for recording this program . . .

MR. GRAVES: That's exactly it. Well, this poem? Oh, yes, if you insist:

207

To evoke posterity
Is to weep on your own grave,
Ventriloquizing for the unborn:
'Would you were present in flesh, hero!
What wreaths and junketings!'

And the punishment is fixed:
To be found fully ancestral,
To be cast in bronze for a city square,
To dribble green in times of rain
And stain the pedestal.

Spiders in the spread beard;
A life proverbial
On clergy lips a-cackle;
Eponymous institutes,
Their luckless architecture.

. . . in case you or anybody doesn't know what 'eponymous' means, it's a four-bit word. Vanderbilt . . .

MR. NEWMAN: Vanderbilt University . . .

MR. GRAVES: Vanderbilt University is an eponymous
institution; so is Duke University. And there are a whole
lot of other *eponymia* around, such as Kennedy Airport—
it used to be Idlewild, when I knew it first. Now it's an
eponymous institution.

Two more dates of life and birth
For the hour of special study
From which all boys and girls of mettle
Twice a week play truant
And worn excuses try.

It has some more verses; let's forget about them. What
else did you want to say?

MR. NEWMAN: I'd like you, if you would, to read *Spite of
Mirrors*.

MR. GRAVES: Oh, this is . . .

208

MR. NEWMAN: Malcolm Muggeridge asked you whether the women to whom your poems were written were real or imaginary?

MR. GRAVES: Yes.

MR. NEWMAN: Well, this is certainly a poem about a woman; I don't know whether real or imaginary . . .

MR. GRAVES: Yes, well—she was partly Mexican, partly Basque and partly Italian.

O what astonishment if you
Could see yourself as others do,
Foiling the mirror's wilful spite
That shows your left cheek as the right
And shifts your lovely crooked smile
To the wrong corner! But meanwhile
Lakes, pools and puddles all agree
(Bound in a vast conspiracy)
To reflect only your stern look
Designed for peering in a book—
No easy laugh, no glint of rage,
No thoughts in passionate pilgrimage,
Nor start of guilt, nor rising fear,
Nor premonition of a tear.

And how, with mirrors, can you keep
Watch on your eyelids closed in sleep?
How judge which profile to bestow
On a new coin or cameo?
How, from two steps behind you, stare
At your firm nape discovered bare
Of ringlets as you bend and reach
Transparent pebbles from the beach?
Love, if you long for a surprise
Of self-discernment, hold my eyes
And plunge deep down in them to see
Sights never long withheld from me.

I didn't read that very well. Never mind. It was well-intended.

MR. NEWMAN: Mr. Graves, are you writing songs now?

MR. GRAVES: Am I writing songs? Yes. I was asked the other day to write a carol for *The New York Times*, and thought, 'That's a silly thing to do', and then I . . . you see, I now spend a lot of my time picking up olives. It's the season, and picking is very good for the back, and keeps your fingers greasy. Also it keeps your mind working, because half the time you don't have to think. And—what was I talking about?

MR. NEWMAN: You were talking about writing a song.

MR. GRAVES: Yes. So I found myself writing a carol as I was picking olives. And—I don't know how long other people are going to write carols. Carol-making is rather an out of date job. Wait a moment. Yes, here it is.

MR. NEWMAN: I don't believe it, but . . . (*laughs*)

MR. GRAVES:

> Shepherds armed with staff and sling,
>   Ranged along a steep hillside,
> Watch for their anointed King
>   By all prophets prophesied—
> *Sing patience, patience,*
> *Only still have patience!*
>
> Hour by hour they scrutinize
>   Comet, planet, planet, star,
> Till the oldest shepherd sighs:
>   'I am frail and he is far.'
> *Sing patience* etc.
>
> 'Born, they say, a happy child;
>   Grown, a man of grief to be,
> From all careless joys exiled,
>   Rooted in eternity.'
> *Sing patience* etc.
>
> Then another shepherd said:
>   'Yonder lights are Bethlehem;

210

There young David raised his head
    Destined for the diadem.'
Sing patience etc.

Cried the youngest shepherd: 'There
    Our Redeemer comes tonight,
Comes with starlight on his hair,
    With his brow exceeding bright,'
Sing patience etc.

'Sacrifice no lamb nor kid,
    Let such foolish fashions pass;
In a manger find him hid,
    Breathed upon by ox and ass.'
Sing patience etc.

'Dance for him and laugh and sing,
    Watch him mercifully smile,
Dance although tomorrow bring
    Every plague that plagued the Nile!'
Sing patience, patience,
Only still have patience!

Well, now, that is old-fashioned, isn't it? But it takes a great deal of patience to write it nowadays.

MR. NEWMAN: And what about the music?

MR. GRAVES: I didn't write the music. I've only once written music for a song, and then the words were by someone else. There's often melody at the back of one's head, but the control of words in a song is an astonishing feat, because one must consider the music and the singer at the same time. Besides, the song is incomplete without the music, and the music is incomplete without the song. The two best English song-writers, Dowland and Campion, both wrote their own words to their own music, so that they really went together.

MR. NEWMAN: Mr. Graves, about poetry: children are exposed to poetry almost as soon as they go to school.

But very little poetry seems to remain in the lives of ordinary people. As you have said, it's generally accepted that it's almost impossible for a poet to support himself by writing poetry. Why has poetry faded from the lives of ordinary people, in the so-called advanced countries?

MR. GRAVES: It's a matter of climate, physical and moral. Very few poets have written poems in cities, probably because the ancient poetic tradition is closely bound up with trees, fruits, flowers and stars. City-dwellers seldom see any stars: they get blotted out by the polluted sky. Too many tourists come here to Majorca and ask me 'What tree is that?' They don't known the difference between an elm and a birch. They have often never seen orange trees, and when they see oranges growing on mine they plead: 'Oh, may I pick an orange off a tree?' It's sad.

MR. NEWMAN: Is technological advance destructive of poetry? Is it a bad thing for poetry that we have landed men on the moon?

MR. GRAVES: Between you and me, it's the most shocking thing that's ever happened, since Alexander the Great cut the Gordian Knot—when was it?—in about 336 or 334? The Gordian knot? Well, it was a particularly magical knot that was tied on an oxcart at Gordium in Asia Minor. It had been prophesied that whoever could undo the knot, would be Lord of Asia. Alexander fiddled about for hours, but couldn't untie it. The real point about that knot was that it spelt out a holy name in knot-language. You will find examples of knot-language on ancient Irish arabesques and the British Druids used to exchange messages in knot-language. . . . But Alexander was no Druid and couldn't be bothered to study their mysteries. So he took his dagger and cut the knot right across. This was his studied contempt for all religious secrets, and one of the worst moments in history. . . . Alexander went out East and won great

212

victories, but soon came back and drank himself to death. His own country fell to pieces, too. Everything fell to pieces.

MR. NEWMAN: What you're saying then, Mr. Graves, is that we should allow some mystery to survive.

MR. GRAVES: Mystery cannot help surviving. But the point is that once one starts publicizing a mystery, one is heavily punished. I don't mean you personally, Mr. Newman, because I'm sure you wouldn't.

MR. NEWMAN: Thank you very much.

MR. GRAVES: You have only put yourself in the position of asking questions; and put me in the embarrassing position of trying to give you answers.

MR. NEWMAN: Yes, sir. And thank you for the answers, Mr. Graves.